THE LIBRARY
ST. MARY'S COLLEGE OF MARYLAND
ST. MARY'S CITY, MARYLAND 20686

Cen Shen

Twayne's World Authors Series

William Schultz, Editor

University of Arizona

TWAS 694

Cen Shen

By Marie Chan
University of Arizona

Twayne Publishers · Boston

Cen Shen

Marie Chan

Copyright © 1983 by G.K. Hall & Company
All Rights Reserved
Published by Twayne Publishers
A Division of G. K. Hall & Company
70 Lincoln Street
Boston, Massachusetts 02111

Printed on permanent/durable acid-free paper and bound in the United States of America.

Library of Congress Cataloging in Publication Data

Chan, Marie, 1944-
  Cen Shen.

  (Twayne's world authors series; TWAS 694)
  Bibliography: p. 154
  Includes index.
  1. Ts'en, Ts'an, 715-770. 2. Poets, Chinese—Biography. I. Title. II. Series.
PL2677.T7Z6   1983   895.1'13   83-155
ISBN 0-8057-6541-7

Contents

About the Author

Preface

Chronology

    CHAPTER ONE
    The Life and Times of Cen Shen   1

    CHAPTER TWO
    The Poems   19

    CHAPTER THREE
    Poetry in a Social Context   43

    CHAPTER FOUR
    Frontier Poetry   72

    CHAPTER FIVE
    Evaluations   111

Abbreviations Used in Notes and
References and Bibliography   131

Notes and References   133

Selected Bibliography   154

Index   158

About the Author

Marie Chan was born in Chongqing, China, and educated in England and the United States. She took her doctorate in Comparative Literature from the University of California, Berkeley, and is currently teaching at the University of Arizona. Her research interests are primarily in the literature of the Tang dynasty and in comparative East-West literary relations. She is the author of Kao Shih (Twayne Publishers, 1978), as well as articles that have appeared in various scholarly journals including the Journal of the American Oriental Society and Comparative Literature.

Preface

Native Chinese criticism has long acknowledged Cen Shen as a great poet of what is perhaps the great age of Chinese poetry. Since the Song dynasty he is recognized for consummate technical mastery and for novelty of style and theme. More recently, Cen's poems on Central Asia and the desert frontier of the Tang empire have attracted considerable critical interest. He is regarded now as an original genius who seems unshackled by many of the constraints of classical Chinese poetry.

With the exception of a sprinkling of standard "anthology" entries and essays by Arthur Waley and Stephen Owen, Cen Shen, like many of his peers in Chinese poetry, is virtually unknown in the West. The studies and translations of Cen's distinguished contemporaries that have appeared in recent years are just beginning to fill the significant gap in the West's knowledge of one of the most remarkable periods of poetic florescence in literature. This volume endeavors to introduce Cen Shen to students of Chinese as well as general literature. It contains a brief biography of the poet, translations and commentaries of seventy-four selected compositions out of the four hundred extant poems by Cen Shen, and a concluding survey of the critical responses to his poetry. Rather than underline the recent critical identification of Cen with the "frontier school" of poetry, my selection aims at a representation of the full range of Cen's oeuvre. In my discussions of, and notes on, the poems, I have tried to consider the interest of the general reader as well as the student of Chinese literature. Hence I tend to emphasize those poetic qualities that can be retrieved in translation over other, equally vital properties that can only partially survive that process; thus discussion of the sound of the poetry is kept at a minimum and the annotations are abbreviated to what is necessary for the understanding of a poem in responsible translation. In the translations themselves, I place fidelity to the original over facility of rendition. The <u>pinyin</u> system of romanization is used throughout with two exceptions: the city of Taipei and all forms of the word "Tao." References given after each poem specify the page number in the <u>Complete Tang Poetry</u> (<u>Quan Tangshi</u>).

Marie Chan

University of Arizona

Chronology

715   Birth.

729–734   Reclusion at Songyang near Loyang.

734   As an alternative to taking the jinshi examinations, submitted samples of his works to the examiners; these were not accepted.

744   Received the jinshi degree; appointed Administrator of Supplies for the Crown Prince's Bodyguards.

749   Joined the staff of Gao Xianzhi, Regional Commander of Anxi.

751   Gao Xianzhi appointed to Wuwei. In the fifth month he was defeated in the Battle of Talas. Cen returned to Chang'an.

754   Appointed to the staff of Feng Changqing as Judicial Investigator, Administrative Officer of Anxi and Beiting and some time later, Assistant Commissioner of Expenses for Yixi and Beiting.

757   Joined Suzong's temporary headquarters at Fengxiang; appointed Omissioner. On 13 November loyalist forces recaptured Chang'an. Suzong and his court returned to the capital the following month.

759   Appointed Chamberlain of Activity and Repose in the third month; transferred to Senior Officer of Guozhou the next month.

762   Recalled to Chang'an as Vice-president of the Secretariat of the Crown Prince and Censor in the Court of Palace Affairs. In the tenth month, accompanied the Prince of Yong's campaign against Shi Chaoyi at Shanzhou. Returned

	to Chang'an toward the end of the year as Assistant Secretary of the Board of Sacrifice.
763	Appointed Assistant Secretary of the Board of Merit.
764	Promoted to Head of the Board of Forestry.
765	Transferred to Head of the Board of Arsenal. Appointed Prefect of Jiazhou; his departure delayed by a rebellion in Shu.
766	Joined the staff of Du Hongjian, Regional Commander of Jiannan and Xichuan, as Head of the Bureau of Military Affairs. Arrived in Chengdu in the summer and shortly afterwards reached his post at Jiazhou.
768	Left his post at Jiazhou in the seventh month and headed for home. His passage cut off by local rebels at Rongzhou. Returned to Chengdu and took up temporary residence there.
770(?)	Death

Chapter One
The Life and Times of Cen Shen

The Cen family of Nanyang (in modern Henan) was a distinguished clan. In the early years of the Tang dynasty it produced three noted ministers, a fact that Cen Shen proudly mentions: "Of the six generations since the founding of the Tang, our family has had three chief ministers."[1] They were Cen Wenben (595-645), the poet's great-grandfather and a literatus of note, Cen Changqian (d. 691), his grand-uncle who served Gaozong and the Empress Wu, and Cen Xi (d. 713), his uncle and Ruizong's chief minister. The last two men were involved in court intrigues which eventually brought misfortunes to the family. Changqian was imprisoned and executed together with his sons for opposing the powerful Wu clan and then Cen Xi was implicated in the Taiping princess's plot against her nephew Li Longji (posthumous temple name, Xuanzong). As a result he too was put to death, and more than ten members of the Cen family who were employed in the government at the time were disgraced.[2]

The incident involving the Taiping princess happened in 713, just a few years before the poet's birth.[3] During Cen's childhood the family greatness had already become a fond if still vivid memory. Years later as a young candidate for the jinshi ("Presented Scholar") degree, Cen reminded the world of his noble ancestors:

> At dusk they would leave the yellow doors of the premier's council chamber and at dawn they would hurry to the purple gates of the imperial city. Their embellished wheel hubs illumined the road; their jade rein ornaments startled the dust. Our kin were placed in lofty assemblies. Songs and gongs swelled in early spring. The young and the old were scarlet sashed officials. Great and glorious, there were more than ten of them.[4]

Cen Shen's father, Zhi, held a number of provincial appointments, the last being the prefectship of Jinzhou (modern southern Shanxi). He died when Shen was still a

1

boy, leaving the family in rather straitened circumstances. Cen Shen was one of five sons, and at least one other brother also gained a reputation for letters. There are several poems addressed to Cen Kuang from Liu Changqing (710?-785?). Du Fu (712-770), one of Shen's great friends, describes the Cen brothers as men who relished the unusual and Wang Changling (698?-765) speaks of the "two scions of the Cen house whose surpassing brilliance is hard to emulate."[5]

Like most Chinese literati Cen wanted to remember himself as a precocious youngster. He claims that he learned to read at the age of five and to compose at nine.[6] Du Que (ca. 800), the first compiler of his works, observes that in his youth Cen applied himself assiduously to his studies and became well read in the histories. Following Cen Zhi's untimely death, Shen and the rest of the family returned to their estate near Songyang (modern Dengfeng, Henan). Cen Shen seemed to have lived on both the eastern slopes of Mt. Song (also known as Taisihi) and on the western slopes (called Shaoshi), some seventy li apart from each other. Early manhood was spent in retirement and cultivation of learning. The many eremitic poems dating from this early period[7] show him assuming the typical guise of the scholar-recluse. This was not an uncommon practice among the young men of his class. Li Bo (701-762) and Meng Haoran (689-740) were just two of Cen's great contemporaries who adopted for a time the life-style of the gentleman living in retirement. By the Tang such a practice, far from precluding the possibility of future preferment, had actually become one of the means toward achieving that goal. In a wry mood, the great Taoist patriarch Sima Chengzhen (655-735) had described eremitism as the shortcut to office.[8] Indeed the precedent set by Zhuge Liang (181-234) and the other talented men summoned out of retirement to serve the state had resulted in a curious extension of the ends of reclusion; aspiring officials often elected to live as hermits with every expectation that when they did enter officialdom, their fame as former eremites would only strengthen their credentials. Cen Shen's attraction to the eremitic ideals at this point of his life was no doubt genuine. Yet like so many of his contemporaries, he embraced these ideals without ever excluding the eventuality that he would also pursue the opposite position of worldly commitment.

Cen probably wanted that future to come soon. As Wang

Wei (701-761) observes: "In time of order one seldom goes into reclusion; / When the Way prevails, how can one leave the world?"[9] Xuanzong's brilliant early reign during the kaiyuan (713-741) era provided no ethical justification for withdrawing from public life. So at twenty Chinese years (sui), Cen presented to the examination authorities, as an accepted alternative to taking the jinshi examination, some of his compositions.[10] But he failed to gain official recognition with this move. The next few years were spent in the environs of the two capitals. He married sometime around 742,[11] and he traveled extensively in the northern provinces, visiting such places of historical interest as Handan and Daliang. Touring the empire was a fashionable pursuit among young literati. Li Bo's and Du Fu's youthful travels are celebrated in Chinese literary history. The unspoken purpose of such peregrinations was to widen one's circle of acquaintances and patrons with a view of promoting one's official career. And indeed Cen did meet such gifted literati as Liu Changqing and Wang Changling. It would appear that he became more than a passing acquaintance to Wang; a poignant farewell composed when Wang was banished to Jiangning about 742 exhorts him to patience. "The hidden dragon coils in the depth, / The yellow crane is tardy in its flight." Hidden dragons and cranes are conventional symbols of the unemployed worthy. Cen continued to send letters to Wang Changling in exile. On one occasion a new jinshi returning in triumph to his Jiangning home was the carrier; Cen rejoiced in the young man's success and looked forward to a new era with the change of reign title to tianbao. The sense of expectancy deepened his sympathy for Wang, who was not included in the general amnesty following the proclamation of the new reign era. "Wang, my brother, is still a disgraced official; / Once again he sees autumn clouds rise in a lonely citadel before the lake." Cen surmises, however, that Wang Changling's heart was "clear as the lake's water," and that he often found consolation in the Taoist canons.[12]

Late in 743 Cen Shen presented himself as a candidate for the jinshi, but before doing so, he submitted a fu or prose-poem entitled "Moved by Past Events."[13] In this composition he refers to Cen Xi's crime: "It was as a result of concerted lies that my uncle, the Duke of Ru'an, was punished." This was probably a shrewd move to expunge any possible prejudice against him because of his family associations. If that was the case, the appeal seemed to have helped for in 744 he placed second in the examination and was appointed Administrator of Supplies in the office of the Crown Prince's Bodyguards. Posts in the Crown Prince's household were not coveted appointments since holders were far removed from the affairs of government. And Cen, no doubt, was more than a little discomfited by the fact that he had to repudiate his eremitic stance for such a lowly office. It was always a little awkward for a self-proclaimed recluse to abandon this position; neediness provided a ready and, perhaps real, reason for returning to the sullied world of men:

1. Inscribed at Gaoguan's Thatched Cottage When I Received My First Appointment

At thirty I received my first post.
My aspirations for office, my many desires
 are exhausted.
I pity myself for having no property;
And dare not feel shame for my lowly office.
My mountain torrent engorges the rustic path;
The flowers in the hills intoxicate my herb trellis.
Because of five piculs of rice,
I have betrayed my fishing rod.[14] (2089)

The penultimate line is an allusion to the georgic poet Tao Qian (365-427), who refused to bend his back for the official salary of five piculs of rice.

An ambitious young man who had looked forward to being in the thick of the political fray could not but have chafed at being relegated to the Crown Prince's entourage. Cen managed to find distraction in the amenities of Chang'an. Among his new friends was Du Fu, who was even less successful in finding a position. At thirty-three sui Du had yet to pass the jinshi examination. We know that the Cen brothers invited Du Fu to an outing at Lake Meipi, some twenty-four miles southwest of Chang'an below the celebrated Mt. Zhongnan. This was how Cen describes the cruise:

2. Floating on Meipi with a Group of Officials from Hu Subprefecture

A vast expanse saturated by the sky's hues.

A depth that reaches the earth's root.
Our boat moves—the city merges with the woods;
The shore widens—upon the water floats a village.
Idle egrets startled by our reed and pipe;
Submerged dragons flank our wine flasks.
Darkness falls, we call our servants,
To light the fire and hasten our returning carriages.
(2084)

Compared with Cen's urbane piece, Du Fu's version is more intense and serious. The uncertain course of the boating trip is seen as a metaphor for the vicissitudes of life itself:

The Song of Meipi

The Cen brothers relish the strange;
They take me afar for an excursion of Meipi.
The world darkening suddenly takes on an unusual hue.
A boundless stretch of billows, a pile of glass.
Into this expanse of glass our boat floats.
The event is different, the elation great, thoughts
 gather anxiously.
The action of alligators, swallowing by whales, are
 no longer known;
But an evil wind or white waves could come most
 lamentably.
Our hosts help in hoisting the brocade sails;
Our boatmen rejoice that the fog has lifted.
Geese and gulls flutter wildly as the song of the
 oars bursts forth;
Strings and pipes come shrilly through the blue sky.
Sunken poles and long cords cannot fathom the deep.
Aquatic leaves and lotus blossoms fresh as if
 scrubbed.
Lo, we're right in the middle of a watery expanse
 so clear.
Below in the boundless waters, Mt. Zhongnan darkens.
Half of the lake's south side suffused with the
 mountain.
Moving shadows wave and waft in great harmony.
Our boat's bulwarks in the dark tap Cloud End
 Temple.
On the face of the water a moon emerges from
 Lantian Pass.
T'is now the time that the black dragon spits the

pearl;
And to the drumbeat of Fengyi, the herd of dragons races.
Ladies of the Xiang and maidens of the Han emerge to sing and dance.
Gilded poles and kingfisher flags in the wavering light.
From time to time we fear that a thunderstorm would come;
In this vast space we don't understand the god's intent.
How short is youth, most inevitable, old age.
Can joy and sorrow ever be too many?[15] (2261)

In his graver and more private moments Cen Shen seemed impatient for official recognition. Repeatedly he refers to the age of thirty, which marks the coming into manhood in traditional China, and he praises other men's ability to win early fame while he himself languished in the office of the Crown Prince's Bodyguards. For five years no promotion came to Cen. In 749 he accepted a secretarial position on the staff of the Korean-born Gao Xianzhi (d. 755),[16] the regional commander of Anxi, with its center at Kucha in modern Xinjiang. Cen's title was Clerk of the Imperial Wuwei Guards of the Right. Because of the expansionist policies of Xuanzong's later reign, serving on the staff of the military governors had become a rather popular alternative to the tedium of an insignificant civil appointment that carried little likelihood of advancement. Du Fu and Gao Shi (706?-765) were just two of Cen's frustrated contemporaries who worked for a time on the staffs of military commanders. Holders of such offices were not the objects of envy. For the medieval Chinese, leaving the Middle Kingdom for the northern hinterland was tantamount to exile. And there is more than a hint of resignation in Cen's tone when he writes in reference to his departure for Anxi: "When a man has gained neither fame nor fortune at thirty, he can hardly pore over his studies all day long."[17]

In 751 Gao Xianzhi returned to Chang'an to report to the emperor and was transferred to the Governor of Wuwei (modern Liangzhou, Gansu) and regional commander of Hexi, replacing the stepbrother of An Lushan, An Sishun. His staff, including Cen Shen, was probably pleased with the transfer, which placed them in greater proximity to the capital. They proceeded to Wuwei, expecting their commander to join them there soon. An Sishun, however, managed to have the tribes under his jurisdiction insist upon his retention. Gao was then given the title of Great Yulin General. In the fourth month of that year, the Arabs attacked several Chinese garrisons. Gao Xianzhi was ordered to lead an army of thirty thousand men, made up of both Chinese and non-Chinese, against the Arabs. He met them at Talas, some two hundred miles east of Samarkand. During the siege, the Karluk Turks, who were nominally under Chinese suzerainty, revolted and joined the enemy. Defeated, Gao fled east.

Unemployed now, Cen Shen returned to Chang'an that summer and spent the next two years there. He renewed his friendship with Du Fu, for we know that he visited, most probably in the autumn of 752, the famous Buddhist Temple of Compassionate Mercy with Du and three other men of letters, Gao Shi, Chu Guangxi (jinshi 726), and Xue Ju (b. 702?). The poem which Cen wrote on that occasion expresses a desire to give up public life and to devote himself to Buddhism. That this statement is more of a literary convention than real resolve became clear in 754 when he attached himself to the staff of Gao Xianzhi's successor at Anxi, Feng Changqing (d. 755), who was also given the command of the Protectorate of Beiting (Besbaliq, Zungharia) and Yixi (Hami). Cen was appointed Judicial Investigator with the rank of Censor in the Chayuan (one of the three censorial halls), as well as Administrative Officer of Anxi and Beiting. On his way to the far west, he composed a graceful quatrain:

3. Crossing Long Mountain on My Way to Beiting, I Think of Home

Heading westwards to Luntai, a myriad miles away,
I know that letters from home will grow fewer
   with each passing day.
Parrots of Long Mountain, if you can speak,
Report to my kin with this message.[18] (2106)

Sometime later Cen was made Assistant Commissioner of Expenses for Yixi and Beiting.[19] Much of his time was spent at Luntai (modern Bugur). His superior Feng Changqing[20] conducted a series of military expeditions, and Cen wrote the obligatory verses to celebrate his exploits. Some of these pieces, such as the "Song of Luntai" and "The Song of Running Horse River," are justly famous. The private verses addressed to departing friends which describe the Central Asian landscape are of equal interest. The frontier years were perhaps Cen's most creative period. Often he expresses a typical Chinese sense of alienation: "In sorrow it is hard to pass the days. / My return is still many years away."[21] The disjointed seasonal and diurnal cycle of the frontier, when "autumn snow falls yet in spring," and the "morning wind does not cease at night,"[22] was a constant reminder that at the ripe age of forty success had still not come to him. Yet Cen had an adventurous spirit and his zest for the unusual eased his longing for home. The area under Feng Changqing's jurisdiction was considerably larger than that which Gao Xianzhi controlled. Consequently, Cen found himself constantly moving on official business between Anxi and Beiting through some of the most awesome scenery of the western region. He wrote about the strange desertscape of the Fire Mountains in the Turfan Depression as well as the robust dances and music of Central Asia. He was especially enraptured by a twirling dance known as "Like the Lotus Flower Spear Dance"; carried away by enthusiasm, he pronounces it as unlike "anything the world has ever seen." As for the music, he claims that the tribal pipes made such perennial Chinese favorites as "Plucking the Lotus" and "Falling Plum Blossoms" sound cacophonous. The crude life of the frontier garrison fascinated this man of letters. His poems describe days of hard toil against an inclement nature and nights of hard drinking with stout companions. There were times when the hot desert wind would blow even in winter, evaporating the sweat no sooner than it streamed down the men's weary backs. And there were nights of rowdy merriment, such as the party given by a General Gai (poem 74); it was held in a cozy room fitted in tribal style with rugs and wall hangings. Household servants, resplendent in purple sashes and gold badges, served wine from jade flasks and game delicacies from gold vessels. Dressed in elaborately embroidered purple gauze jackets, two female entertainers sang for them and partnered them in a dice game called <u>shupu</u>. The formality and restraint of the Middle Kingdom were forgotten as the guests were plied with wine. Intoxicated, they "vied for the wine cup, clamoring and shouting."

    The far west garrisons must have learned of An Lushan's rebellion shortly after it began in the eleventh month of 755. Feng Changqing was recalled to the court immediately. Cen Shen, whose civil qualifications were of little use at this moment of crisis, was not invited to return with him. Officially he remained Assistant Commissioner for Expenses for Yixi and Beiting. In reality, however, he was leading a life of semiretirement. He distracted himself with bucolic hobbies. "My job leaves me with a great deal of leisure and in the garden of my office, I plant herbs, make miniature hills and install a pond." One day Cen received from a colleague a rare flower which grows only in the Tianshan Mountains. The flower, which he calls the Youbenlou blossom, thrilled him since it was like no other blossom that he had previously seen. "Its strange fragrance pervades the air; its lovely colors adorn our surroundings." It is a fitting metaphor for himself, living in oblivion in a remote frontier town while momentous events were shaping the course of the empire. "I sigh in admiration of the flower. Why do you not bloom in the Middle Kingdom but are, rather, sequestered in the distant frontier, thus permitting the peony to be valued and the hibiscus to be prized? And how is your fate different from the worthy who is not received by his lord but is expelled to the wilderness." Cen arrives at a philosophic consolation: "Heaven has no prejudice, the yin and yang are impartial. How can growth be denied because the place is remote or fragrance cease because there is no man?"[23] Cen shared the values of his society; above all else, he wanted to inherit the mantle of distinguished service which his forbears had worn. Yet in his poetry he never dwelt upon his frustrations with the impassioned single-mindedness of so many Chinese poets. His curiosity for new sights and new experiences and his search for new expressions distracted him from the depth of melancholia that characterizes so much of great Chinese poetry since Qu Yuan's (343?-278) poem the "Lisao" (Encountering sorrow).

In the late summer of 756, the rebels captured Chang'an and the situation became yet more grave. Early the following year Cen made his way back home. The court had assembled at Fengxiang, some one hundred miles west of Chang'an, under a new emperor, Li Yu (posthumous temple name, Suzong). Cen found a number of old acquaintances there and a friend in the person of Du Fu. A memorial submitted by Du, dated the twelfth day of the sixth month, recommended Cen for a post and cited his "perspicacity of judgment and rectitude of deliberation."[24] Cen was subsequently appointed Omissioner of the Secretariat, a post that was nominally higher than that held by Du Fu, who was a Reminder. He was now forty-three sui and had reached the seventh rank, second class with an appointment that gave him neither prestige nor influence. He describes his disappointment in two poems to which he gave the old folk-song (yuefu) title of "Following the Army on Campaign." In the second piece he seems to attribute his failure to gain preferment to ignorance of the arts of war:

**Following the Army on Campaign
(At the time I was in the
imperial retinue at Fengxiang)**

I venture to sorrow for my life.
At forty I am not yet old.
One morning civil war began;
Each day our lives uncertain.
The Tartar troops have taken Chang'an;
Within palace chambers wild weeds grow.
I'm heartbroken for the trees of Wuling;
I no longer see the capital's boulevards.
My sovereign is with the marching troops;
Arms and horses are everywhere.
The Tartar rebels are not yet quelled;
Ernestly the many commanders subjugate them.
Recently I heard of Xianyang's fall;
In the massacre all swept clean.
A mass of corpses piled like a hillock;
Oozing blood swells this land of Feng and Hao.
Shields and spears impede my homeland;
Jackals and tigers all over the citadel's walls.
Villages and hamlets without any man.
Desolate the mulberry and date trees.
The scholar has a far reaching plan,
But there is no place to express his innermost
   thoughts.
Alone, there is a man lamenting for his time;
Lifting his head he wails to the blue sky.

Had I known that I would live in warring
   times,
I would have cheated in my studies as a boy.
I regret not learning to draw the bow,
And shoot the wild Tartars in the east.
By chance I walk in the rank of advisors;
Mistakenly I head towards the cinnabar steps.
Unable to assist my sovereign,
In vain I was born a man.
Clasping my sword, I sorrow on the road of

>   the world;
>   Lamenting with a song I weep for the good
>   strategy.
>   Merit and patrimony, too late now.
>   Glancing at the mirror, I sorrow for my white
>   beard.
>   All my life, I've cherished loyalty;
>   I dare not consider my insignificant
>   person.[25] (2047)

On the Double Ninth festival that year, traditionally an occasion for family reunion, Cen thought of his home in Chang'an and composed the celebrated quatrain in which he imagined that his garden was now a battlefield (Poem 31). He could not have known that he would be seeing his home before the year was out. In the tenth month the Tang forces inflicted a major defeat upon the rebels and recovered the capital. Suzong was able to return in triumph the following month, bringing with him hopes for renewed stability and prosperity.

Cen, no doubt, shared the general optimism. He now joined a distinguished group of literati who were employed in the restored court, a group which included Jia Zhi (718-772), Wang Wei, and Du Fu. One day the four met after attending the morning audience at Daming Palace. Jia composed a poem celebrating that daily ceremony and he then invited his three colleagues to respond with matching verses. Such verses naturally lend themselves more to displays of poetic virtuosity than to expressions of deep feelings. The four compositions on the morning audience at Daming Palace are limited by the constraints of public poetry. Even so, the verve with which Cen and his colleagues described the court ceremony reflects their relief over the newly restored order and their optimism that the war was now behind them.

For any man of ambition this was a challenging time. Gao Shi, a fellow literatus and acquaintence who is often discussed in conjunction with Cen in later poetics, came to high estate during this period.[26] Cen himself, however, failed to distinguish himself. He languished at the Secretariat in a post which placed him tantalizingly close to the emperor's person but which gave him no influence in the decisions of government. Although the duties of the omissioner and the reminder were formally defined as to advise the emperor on oversights in public affairs, their actual role had largely become a ceremonial one of attending upon the emperor on state occasions. Cen expresses his sense of helplessness in a poem to Du Fu, who, it will be recalled, held a similar position as Reminder in the Chancellery:

6. To Reminder Du of the Chancellery

With joint strides we hurry towards the cinnabar steps;
In separate offices I am confined to the Purple Myrtle bureau.[27]
At dawn I follow the Sword of State and enter;
By dusk, charmed by imperial fragrance, I leave.
My white hairs sorrow for the flowers' fall;
Blue clouds envy the birds' flight.
In this sagely reign there are few omissions;
I feel my memorials becoming scarce. (2064)

The poem contains a number of double entendres: the word "confined" (xian) describes the physical barrier that separated himself at the Secretariat from Du Fu in the Chancellery as well as confinement in the sense of lack of advancement. Because he was thus circumscribed, Cen envied the flight of the birds; this again is an ambiguous image since "blue cloud" is both a marker for high estate and for eremitism. But it is the last couplet which has generated the most heated discussion.[28] Cen's statement that memorials were superfluous because there was no room for improvement is indeed outrageous in view of the fact that he was referring to a court struggling to return to normalcy after a serious rebellion. Scholars of later ages have censured him for what would seem to be fulsome subservience. It is possible that they have overlooked the dark irony of the statement. Cen himself could not have been unaware of the impropriety of his comment. He may be hinting at the futility of submitting memorials that were bound to be either overlooked or rejected. A remark made the year following his transfer to Guozhou that "no one even glances at my memorials"[29] seems to support this reading.

Cen's curious concluding statement might also have been meant as a gentle warning to Du Fu to be less zealous and pressing in his own memorials to the throne. We know that Du had been working deep into the night preparing reports and that the court was finding him an increasing nuisance.[30]

In the summer of that year, he was transferred to a provincial post following the fall of his patron, Fang Guan. If Cen had intended to admonish Du Fu to discretion, then Du's response is most interesting.

Responding to Omissioner Cen

> Inviolate, the clear Forbidden Gates;
> Leaving the court, we return by different
>   routes.
> You, Sir, follow the ministers;
> I head east of Solar Floriate Gate.
> Tender the willow branches, jasper green;
> Lovely the pistils, so red.
> My friend has composed lovely lines,
> Which he alone sends to the white haired
>   oldster.[31] (2414)

The conventions of the verse response require acknowledgment of the sentiments and expressions of the initial poem in as full a manner as possible. Du Fu's first four lines faithfully answer Cen's poem: "return by different routes" is in response to Cen's "in separate offices," while "Forbidden Gates" are antiphonal to "cinnabar steps" and the "Solar Floriate Gate" leading to the Chancellery answers Cen's "Purple Myrtle Office" of the Secretariat. Cen's reference to falling blossoms is matched by the image of red pistils and the white hair which Cen finds on his head is echoed by Du Fu. Yet Du does not acknowledge Cen's most provocative comment in the final couplet. His silence from across the centuries still intrigues.

After Du Fu was removed to Huazhou in the summer of 758, Cen remained in Chang'an for a few more months before a similar order came to him. Prior to his removal from the capital, he registers his sense of frustration and despair in another artfully worded poem:

7. Working in the West Wing[32]

> Layered clouds over the West Wing unfold with
>   the morning radiance.
> Scattered showers from the northern mountain
>   dot our court robes.
> Willow shade before a myriad gates joins the
>   blue volutes;

Flower fragrance within the three chambers
pervades the Purple Myrtle Office.
At dawn upright tablets accompany the file
of courtiers;
By dusk a drooping whip allows my horse
to amble home.
The official is stupid, he laments his white
hair.
Better for him to retire to a rustic cottage
under the cliffs. (2097)

The morning splendor, a harbinger of the stately affairs of the day, is abruptly shattered in line 6, which depicts a listless and disheartened official returning from the court. The poem concludes with a bitter statement of frustration.

His own professions of idleness notwithstanding, Cen was described by Du Que as having been more diligent about his duties than was actually good for him: "he submitted manifold memorials guiding the statesmen and glib-tongued ministers." In the spring of 759, Cen was removed to Chamberlain of Activity and Repose,[33] a sixth-rank post. A month later he learned of his appointment to Senior Officer of Guozhou, midway between Chang'an and Loyang. This was probably one of those promotions to provincial posts whereby the court could rid itself of difficult officials. Cen himself seems to have taken the new appointment as a demotion.[34] The three years at Guozhou augmented his weariness with official life. In a poem sent to his Chang'an friends he complained about the trivia which filled his days: "For some time now I have given up all writing, / All day long I am unrolling documents and records."[35] The following piece again describes his frustration:

8. Assisting in the Commandery I Think of My Old Friends

In the spring of the third month of the year jihai (759), I was transferred from Omissioner to Chamberlain. In the fourth month of summer I was appointed Senior Officer of Guozhou. Just then I saw the autumn grass and the coming of the cool wind again. In former times Lord Huan Tan left as Magistrate of Liu'an[36] and was unhappy. Now I know why. Saddened by the trivia of the prefecture, I remember the ease of the Secretariat. I present this to my old friends of both the Chancellery and the Secretariat.

> Fortunate in being permitted to go to the purple chamber,
> I remember still attending before the cinnabar steps.
> My historical brush is esteemed for being forthright.
> My memorials, no one glances at.
> All my life I've believed in myself;
> In old age, why such lowliness?
> My peers have all attained advancement;
> Lacking talent I alone lag behind.
> On the locust in the courtyard, roosting birds bustle;
> In the grass by the steps, night insects lament.
> My white hairs now are countless;
> Blue clouds have not yet come. (2101)

Cen Shen was recalled to the capital in 762, when he was appointed concomitantly Vice President of the Secretariat of the Crown Prince and Censor in the Court of Palace Affairs. He was subsequently transferred in rapid succession to Assistant Secretary of the Bureaus of Sacrifice and then of Merit. A short while later he was promoted to the fifth rank, first class, with an appointment as Head of the Bureau of Forestry and then of the Bureau of Arsenal.[37] He refers to this series of transfers one autumn evening in a poem sent to a neighbor, but unfortunately he gives no clue as to the reasons behind the changes:

9. Quietly Elated as I Read on an Autumn Evening, I Present This To Secretary Li of the Bureau of War

> The years slip away, now I am in my robust forties.
> Alas, my hair already white when I became a bureau chief.
> The rain dampens the lichens, invading the steps so green;
> Autumn sweeps over the paulownia trees, covering the wells in yellow.
> A startled cicada understands, it seeks a high tree;
> The wandering wild goose returns, weary of late travel.

> Reading my scrolls I try to pierce my neighbor's walls;
> His lamp, so lovely, may lend me light. (2096)

Cen remained in Chang'an until 765, except for a brief period in 762 when he accompanied the Prince of Yong, the future Emperor Dezong, on a campaign against the rebel Shi Chaoyi. While he had celebrated Feng Changqing's victories copiously in verse, no poem has come down to us from this expedition.

In 765[38] Cen was appointed Prefect of Jiazhou (modern Yueshan, Sichuan), a second-grade prefecture of some twenty-five thousand households. Cen could not reach his post immediately because of a local rebellion which followed the assassination of the regional commander by a subordinate. In the second month of the following year, the great soldier-statesman Du Hongjian (709-769) was appointed regional commander of Jiannan and Xichuan and entrusted with the task of quelling the rebels. Cen joined his staff as Head of the Bureau of Regional Military Affairs and Censor in the Court of Palace Affairs. Together they set off but were stalled at Liangzhou (modern southern Shaanxi) from the spring until early summer. When they managed to reach Chengdu, little was accomplished by Du Hongjian, who merely recommended, prior to returning to Chang'an the following spring, that the rebels be officially appointed to the posts they had lawlessly seized two years earlier.

Free now to leave for his post at Jiazhou, Cen set off sometime in the summer of 767. Always captivated by strange sights, his imagination was whetted by the soaring gorges of Shu:

> 10. My sweat flows as we leave bird paths,
> My gall shatters as I squint upon serpent whirlpools.
> A violent downpour darkens the gorge's mouth,
> As homing clouds throw a net over pines and creepers.
> . . .

He also recalls a storm while sailing down the Yangzi River:

> 11. The gathering waves like hillocks;
> The swirling billows make deep ravines.
> Clouds lower, covering the blossoms by
>   the bank;
> Waters swell, submerging the grass beside

the bank... [39]

Jiazhou itself proved to be a disappointment. Cen notes that his quarters were shabby and that the courtyard before the hall of justice was overgrown with weeds.[40] He remained in this office for no more than a year. In the summer of 768 he left his post and headed homeward, taking the river route to avoid Chengdu and the uncertain peace there. The area was beset by yet another insurrection that spring; Cui Ning, who had revolted against the regional commander the year that Cen received his appointment to Jiazhou and was subsequently appointed provisionary commander, went to Chang'an, leaving his brother in charge. Immediately following his departure, the Prefect of Luzhou revolted but was quickly defeated. He then retreated to his home base with a band of several thousand and blocked off the area. When Cen reached the border between Rongzhou (modern Yibin, Sichuan) and Luzhou, he found his route cut off. He was now stranded on the shores of the Lu River and he despaired for his life: "I sorrow that it has all been in vain; / How can I survive with my life?"[41]

Cen lingered on at Rongzhou for some time, hoping, no doubt, that a passage would open up eventually. He was disappointed and by the spring of 769[42] he had taken up temporary residence in Chengdu. Du Que claims that during this sojourn he composed an essay entitled "Summoning the Shu Visitor to Return"[43] in which he decries the conduct of the rebellious and self-serving officials of the region. If Du Que is right, this would be one of the few prose works Cen left behind. His last datable poem is thought to be a dirge for Pei Mian, who died in the twelfth month of 769. Du Fu, in a poem dating to the twenty-first day of the first month (21 February), 770, the so-called Man's Day (<u>Renri</u>), laments the passing of all his old friends except for two men. Cen was not one of the two. Cen's biographers infer from Du Fu's omission that he died, an exile far from home, sometime between the last month of 769 and the first month of 770.[44] In the Song dynasty, however, Wang Dang (fl. 1101-1110)[45] recounts an episode which may indicate that Cen Shen not only managed to return to Chang'an but died more than a decade later. Wang claims that when Cen was serving as a Director of Decree in the Secretariat during Chang Kun's (729-783) tenure as chief minister between 777 and 779, one of his colleagues, Cui Youfu (721-780), complained about Cen's constant absences from his post.

Chang Kun tried to explain that Cen was ravaged by illness and deserved leniency, whereupon Cui reprimanded the chief minister for hiring such a sick man in the first place. The feud between Chang Kun and Cui Youfu is well documented in both men's official biographies,[46] so that there is some basis for accepting this episode as authentic. If the Cen Shen mentioned in the Song source was indeed our poet, then he must have died after a debilitating illness sometime after 777.

Chapter Two
The Poems

Approximately four hundred of Cen Shen's shi poems have come down to us. Compiled from an unidentified Ming edition and printed in 1703, the Complete Tang Poetry includes 401 pieces, whereas the Sibu congkan edition, based on the 1520 edition printed in Jinan, contains 390 poems.[1] Classified by form,[2] the corpus which Cen left behind yields the following figures:

	Sibu congkan	Complete Tang Poetry
Pentasyllabic ancient style	97	102
Heptasyllabic ancient style	49	51
Pentasyllabic regulated style	170	169
Heptasyllabic regulated style	11	11
Pentasyllabic extended regulated style	12	14
Pentasyllabic quatrain	17	19
Heptasyllabic quatrain	34	35

This and the following two chapters are essentially an anthology of Cen Shen's poems with notes and commentaries. Compilations of poetry are generally arranged in three ways: by form, by content, or by chronology. In the main, Chinese anthologies favor the first system, classifying entries into ancient and recent style works with a subclassification of recent style into regulated verse (lushi) and quatrain (jueju); each form is further subdivided into the pentasyllabic (wuyan) and the heptasyllabic (qiyan) lines. In translations of Chinese poetry, compilation by form loses much of its justification. Most of the characteristics which distinguish and define the different classical poetic forms are lost in Western

19

languages, for no translation can reproduce the differences between the longer and shorter line or the prescribed antithetical and tonal patterns which distinguish recent-style poetry from ancient-style poetry. At best a translation may suggest, perhaps even approximate, a few of these features. Chronological compilation is common in collections consisting of the works of multiple authors spanning one or several dynasties. As a procedure for collecting the works of one man, it permits the reader to discern the development of the poet. Such a compilation is founded upon the accuracy and reliability of biographical materials. While the lives of some major poets are sufficiently well documented to make anthologies arranged by chronology feasible, there are often too many lacunae in the biographies of most Tang poets to entertain such a compilation. Few of the lyric poems contain internal evidence to allow for conclusive dating so that, despite the erudite and oftentimes ingenious inferences of the "chronicle annals" (nianpu), the dating of works composed some twelve hundred years ago remains a conjectural affair. Most studies of individual poets which appear in a Western language are arranged according to theme, perhaps because it is the sole ingredient in poetry that is assured of surviving the brutal process of translation. Some authors and compilers follow the traditional poetic categories such as "palace-style poetry" or "frontier-style poetry," while others create categories to suit their own critical stances. Thematic compilation possesses its own shortcomings. The categories are artificial formulations evolved for critical convenience and they are constantly being overturned by poetic inventiveness. Great poets invariably submit conventional themes to new combinations and configurations. Thus scholars may refer to "frontier poetry" or the "boudoir plaint" as separate entities but the reader of Chinese poetry will often find them intertwined and reinforcing each other in one composition.

Despite these limitations, the last method of compilation is still the most viable. The selection of Cen Shen's poetry in this and the next two chapters is arranged by theme with the form of each work and, whenever possible, the date given under the title.

Reclusion and Nature

As a young man Cen Shen spent a number of years living in retirement in the mountains of Yingyang near Loyang.

These appear to have been halcyon years, and throughout an official career fraught with frustrations and uncertainties, Cen refers constantly to the alternative choice of reclusion and a life lived close to nature. Cen's nature poetry may be divided into two groups: works composed prior to his entry into officialdom and works by a weary official who longs for the private life. The following poem is one of the earliest works in Cen's extant corpus:

12. Looking for Hermit Zhang of Mt. Shaoshi, I Learned That He Has Gone into the Capital with Subprefect Zhou of Yanshi
Pentasyllabic regulated style.
Date: ca. 730

The alchemist of the middle peak,
Yesterday roamed the world of men.
At Leaf County, the wild ducks have all
  left;
Upon Tendril Slope the serpent is back.
Spring clouds gather above the deep waters;
Autumn rain hangs over the empty mountain.
Soundless, at the clear creek,
An idle alchemical oven, empty and unused.
(2087)

Mt. Shaoshi, where Hermit Zhang lived, was also Cen's home around 729-34, while neighboring Yanshi was located west of Loyang. The fruitless visit to an elusive recluse is the subject of numerous Tang poems.[3] Cen's rendition of this familiar theme is playful. Its wit stems from the incongruity between the actual situation and the allusions used to describe it. Hermit Zhang has probably gone to town on some everyday errand. Cen, however, refers to his absence by means of two allusions to transcendence achieved through alchemical elixirs. The wild ducks of Leaf County (modern Xianyang) is an allusion to Wang Qiao of the later Han, who came under suspicion because of his frequent visits to court from his post at Leaf County. It was said that prior to his arrival a pair of ducks would fly from the south. The dragon of Tendril Slope refers to the story of Fei Changfang;[4] in this Chinese counterpart to the tale of the magic carpet, Fei was given a common bamboo rod by a Taoist magician whom he had met in the marketplace. He was told that the rod would take him home in an instant and that, upon reaching his destination, he was to leave it at Tendril Slope. Fei followed these instructions and saw the rod transform into a dragon at the slope. After these allusions, the third couplet returns to the mountain abode of Hermit Zhang. The images of clouds and of rain suspended over high peaks continue to suggest the state of transcendence that is the goal of alchemical experiments. The unused stove is a stock image that implies further concoctions are unnecessary now that its owner has attained the transcendent state. On another level, the abandoned stove objectifies the poet's disappointment and feeling of exclusion. Cen thus interjects the faintest trace of desolation into the tone of playful banter.

On another occasion Cen's journey into the mountain is more fruitful:

13. Upon Visiting Monk Hui of Jingyun from East of Yanshi with Han Zun
Heptasyllabic ancient style.
Date: ca. 730

The old monk of the shady mountain
  understands the Lanka;
The homing travelers of bright Yingyang
  pass from afar.
The mist is deep, the grass moist,
  after last night's rain;
The rain over, autumn wind crosses the
  watercourse.
In the empty mountain, all day long,
  there's little dust;
Over the flat countryside, distant
  sight of tiny passers-by.
At President Wash, a crepuscular bell;
Over Associate Ford, a homing bird.[5]
(2055)

Cen describes the mountain abode of the monk at that wondrous moment when the rain has cleansed the land and replenished its waters. The rain is also a symbol of the act of cleansing defiled thoughts of the "dusty" world. The poem is executed with perfect compositional balance and control. In the first couplet Cen states the theme of returning from a visit to the old monk in the mountain. The remaining three couplets then submit the images of the first pair of lines to amplification and transformation; thus "old" generates "night," "autumn," and "dusk," while "monk" correlates to "little dust" and "temple bell." The image of "homing travelers" is reiterated by "tiny passers-by" and "homing bird." Nothing seems adventitious or random in this poem. The sense of conscious and conscientious art is reinforced by the many antitheses in this ancient-style poem ("The old monk of the shady mountain," matches "The homing travelers of bright Yingyang," while "President Wash" complements "Associate Ford"). Yet Cen is also careful about preserving the distinctness of ancient-style verse; no line is perfectly antithetical to its matching line. If antithesis tends to produce a static effect, the use of "rain" to conclude and to begin two contiguous lines (a rhetorical device known as "linked pearl line") creates a sense of process to offset it.

In the next poem Cen captures another popular moment in the poetry of reclusion - the quiet desolation after parting from a friend.

14. Escorting Jiang Hou to the Head of the River Feng
Pentasyllabic ancient style

You live north of the Feng;
My home, west of the Feng.
Two villages marked by stately trees;
Five hamlets sound with crowing cocks.
We drink wine as the river rain passes;
We play chess until the mountain moon
 sets.
No use now to beat a path to Mr. Jiang,
You're gone, with whom shall I walk
 hand in hand?[6] (2037)

The next four poems treat the theme, so familiar in classical poetry, of the return to nature. Tao Qian's great fu "Homeward Bound" and Wang Wei's equally celebrated "My Villa on Mt. Zhongnan" and "To Vice-prefect Zhang" are examples that come readily to the mind of the reader of Chinese poetry. The return to nature is the statement of the mature man whose public career is achieved and abandoned. The exhilarating moments of discovery of the young man in the mountain retreat are not forgotten; rather they become part of the deepened awareness of the man who has savored the fruit of officialdom and found it distasteful.

In between his public appointments Cen Shen spent intervals out of office. The following account of the "return" describes his retreat on the outskirts of Chang'an:

15. Composed at My Thatched Hut at Twin Peaks, Mt. Zhongnan
Pentasyllabic ancient style.
Date: 751?

My steps retreating, I return to the mountains
 and fields.
My heart at rest, I decline my contemporaries.
In the morning, I return to recline in the
 thatched hut;
Facing only the Twin Peaks.
Exhilarated, I'd freely roam from home;
Wondrous affairs accord with the fine prospect.
I write under the high window;
Day and night I look onto the city.
In former days misled by the world,
I therefore failed my heart's desire.
Long have I parted from the woods and ravines;
Coming now, the pines and firs have grown.
By chance I'm near a monastery here;
Many times I'm able to meet famed monks.
Sometimes I follow the fishermen and foresters,
Not donning my cap and sash all day long.
From the mouth of the precipice a new moon
 ascends;
Stone Gate shatters the gris-green foliage.
Colors near the woods deepen;
Light shimmers, a pond fragments.
I think lovingly of Master Zheng's ravine,
I remember somewhat Yancius's shallow.
Such marvels can still be sought,
But the men are removed by a thousand
 years.[7] (2038)

This long poem delineates a progressively deep consciousness of nature and permanent values. In the first part of the poem, the viewpoint seems to be turned toward the world ("Day and night I look onto the city") and governed by practical observations ("Long have I parted from the woods and ravines, / Coming now the pines and firs have grown."). The most imagistic section is the last eight lines, where the lovely description of the interplay of light and shadow in the moonbeamed night suggests a heightened sense of awareness. The beauty which awakens this state is man's only contact with permanence, for Cen concludes by evoking two celebrated ancient recluses - Yan Guang, a schoolmate of the Emperor Wu of Han who changed his name and became a fisherman to avoid being summoned to office by his old friend, and Zheng Yun, another worthy who spurned high estate. These two men have been dead for many centuries and they can now only be known through the marvels of nature to which they had so determinedly dedicated themselves.

The next three compositions describe visits made by Cen, the public servant, to the retreats of men living in retirement.

16. In Mid-spring I Visit Mr. Yuan's Villa with Several Gentlemen
Pentasyllabic ancient style

South of the suburbs is the gentleman's abode;
A group of peaks arrayed beyond his door.
The fine prospect suddenly entices.
Spring blossoms now most vibrant.
The mountain kitchen is a stove in the bamboos;
The rustic pestle pounds amidst the ivy.
Before our wine, several patches of clouds;
Rolling the blinds, a myriad folds of flowers.
The grotto spring gurgles until dark;
From province and county, I wish to return to
 indolence.
Hues of grass carry the morning rain;
Sound of the rapid mingles with the night bell.
Loving this, I cleanse all vulgar concerns.
To what end do I always defile my visage?
And I have an appointment in the woods;
Changing my mind, my footsteps lead outwards.
 (2038)

Cen gives a poetic account of a day's excursion to the country estate of a friend. The description follows a temporal sequence. The first couplet depicts the visitor's arrival in the prime of day, followed by four lines (4-8) on the feasting. The next couplets describe an evening scene and as darkness obscures all things, the visual images of flora and fauna which fill the first eight lines yield to auditory images. The concluding sentiment of abandoning the dusty world is conventional, even hackneyed, although Cen tries to revive the dead metaphor of the dusty world by evoking the cleansing water image in the preceding lines.

17. On the Lodge of Oldster Zhang at East Rapid, Mt. Taibo: Sent to My Younger Brother, Nephew, and Others
Pentasyllabic ancient style

Over the Wei River the autumn wind passes;
The north wind, how it sough-soughs.
The sky clears, numerous mountains emerge;
The peak of Taibo, the highest of all.
My host is the oldster of East Creek;
Long hairs grow from his ears.
Everyone, far and near, knows he is a
  hundred years old.
His sons and grandsons are white haired men.
In the middle courtyard, over the railing by
  the well,
Is the tree of the Yangtao peach.
At the rocky spring we dine upon fragrant stalks.
For our wine jar, we break a new vat.
I love these bucolic delights,
And begin to perceive the toils of this world.
My journey has many lovely things,
I write this to send to you.[8] (2028)

The poem moves with ease and forthrightness. Classical poetic syntax differs from prose in ways that are hard to retrieve in translation. In the main, poetic syntax is marked by certain grammatical latitude; fluidity of parts of speech permits inversions and other manifestations of scrambled syntax, while licensed omission of particles often entertains purposeful ambiguity. A number of studies[9] have explored the ways in which the great Tang poets have availed themselves of this freedom. The possibilities offered by the poetic grammar are so well realized by Cen Shen's contemporaries that any effort in the opposite direction of the natural idiom is as noteworthy. The diction of this poem is hardly distinguishable from simple classical prose. It

is identifiable as verse only by the presence of rhyme, by
the regular punctuation every five characters and two lines
(11-12) which absence of necessary particles renders
unacceptable as prose.[10] Cen's repudiation of the tortuous
poetic syntax in favor of the straightforward style
complements, of course, the simple life that is proclaimed in
this poem.
    The next piece seems to be a late work:

18. Inscribed in the Abode of the Monk in a Mountain Monastery[11]
Pentasyllabic regulated style

A silhouette by the window wafts with a clump
  of trees;
The shade by the wall contains a peak.
A rustic brazier lights itself in the wind;
A mountain pestle can be pounded in the water.
By dint of study I know my mistakes;
From serving as an official, I hanker for
  indolence.
The lofty monk in the dark cannot be seen.
The moon emerges, I hear only the bell. (2088)

    Recent literary historians generally identify Cen Shen
with the so-called "frontier school" of poetry. With war as
its defining theme, frontier poetry is in many senses the
polar opposite of nature poetry; it addresses itself to
commitment to, rather than withdrawal from, society; the
glory and not the insignificance of fame and high estate.
Tang anthologies, however, point to a different evaluation.
In the compilations from his own dynasty, Cen is represented
by a few nature poems that have received little critical
notice in recent years. It is inevitable that Cen's nature
works be compared with those contemporary poems which are
acknowledged as the most significant examples of this type
of poetry. The comparison is not flattering to Cen, nor,
indeed, is it necessarily judicious to assess his works in
terms of other achievements. On the other hand, an inquiry
into relative merits seems unavoidable since the nature
poetry of this period draws from a shared bank of vocabulary
and conventions that generally marks a retreat from the
particular situation and the individual experience. By the
High Tang the literary formulae for reclusion and life in
nature were so firmly established and so well distilled that

the poems were admired as much for their continued refinement and renewal of a shared frame of reference as for their originality of thought and particularity of moment.

Despite the fact that they draw from a common fount of topoi, Cen Shen's nature verse is easily distinguishable from those of Wang Wei. His "Thatched Hut at Twin Peak" makes essentially the same statement as Wang Wei's "My Villa at Mt. Zhongnan" and "To Vice-prefect Zhang."[12] Yet one searches in vain for those qualities which stamp Wang's poetry and which since his time have become the touchstone of Tang nature poetry. Wang's apparently random and aimless representation seems totally untouched by the cognitive process. Cen Shen's nature poems, on the other hand, are marked by the opposite quality of studied order. His most memorable verses are those in which the natural scene is arranged with a deft and artistic hand. The beauty is not random, but artfully achieved:

> A silhouette by the window sways with a clump
>   of trees;
> The shade by the wall contains a peak . . .
> Before our wine several patches of clouds.
> Rolling back the shades, a myriad folds of
>   flowers. . .

This is "nature to advantage dressed" as the poet strains for the startling observation and the novel perspective. Cen emerges as a master of elegant design wherein the realistic details of trees, mountain peaks, and cloud patches are subordinated to broad patterns and dramatic effect.

Wang Wei's air of unintentional spontaneity and Cen's studied purposefulness reveal themselves also in the perception of themselves and of their return to nature. Wang Wei's statement in "My Villa upon Mt. Zhongnan" is as unforced as it seems unplanned: "In middle age I was somewhat drawn to the Tao, / My home in old age is at the edge of Mt. Zhongnan." Cen's repudiation of the world, by way of contrast, is presented as an act of strong resolve: "My steps retreating, I return to the mountains and fields; / My heart at rest, I decline my contemporaries." In the same poem, Cen's doffing of the official cap and sash is considered, while Wang's sash seems to loosen itself with no human effort: "The wind blew in the pines, loosening my sash." Cen pursues the fishermen and foresters intentionally: "Sometimes I follow the fishermen and foresters." Wang meets them by chance: "Perchance I'd meet an oldster of the woods; / We'd talk and laugh, return has no deadline." Finally, Cen attempts to define the ultimate truth while Wang Wei parries the inquiry with an apparently irrelevant remark which is totally unsatisfactory as propositional statement but which is yet pregnant with implications: "You ask about the ultimate principle, / Fisherman's song enters the shore's deep." In every respect Wang emerges as a passive and uninsistent individual where Cen is striving and resolute.

Cen Shen's repudiation of officialdom is unhesitating and unswerving in his nature verse. His positivism is diametrically contrary to the uncertainty and irresolution that make the poems of the other great contemporary nature poet, Meng Haoran, so affecting. Nowhere does Cen express the ambivalence of "sorrows arising because of dusk" while, at the same time, "exhilaration is leavened by the clear autumn"; or the painfully pleasant anticipation of a friend's tardy arrival: "You surely will come by bedtime, / A long lute awaits at the dodder filled path."[13]

There is little question that Cen Shen's vigorous and resolute view of life is better suited to the poetry of action than of withdrawal. Some aspects of nature, however, furnish an adequate vehicle for the expression of his strong spirit. The depiction of turbulent nature in the following piece is one of the entries for the Tang anthology the Heyue yingling ji (Works of the late valorous spirits of rivers and mountains), compiled about 753:[14]

19. Composed in a Drizzle and Presented to My Friends: Upon Failing to Find Monk Facheng at Cloud End Monastery on Mt. Zhongnan, I Return to the Rocky Splashes of High Crest Pool East and Look Out to the Qin Mountains
Pentasyllabic ancient style

Last night I stayed at Cloud End Monastery;
I returned following the curves of the western pass.
I did not see the monk of the woods.
A drizzle falls upon the pool.
The several peaks all bright kingfisher;
The Qin range alone does not clear.
Stone Drum sometimes sounds;
Can the King of Qin be here?

The water so deep, cutting off the mountain's mouth,
Howling and frothing, it clamors and snorts.
A spurting cliff rains all four seasons;
Adjacent villages thunder on rainy days.
Looking northwards, there's the Chang'an road,
Where dust stirs day and night.
If I visit Zhang Zhongwei —
His rustic gate must be filled with wild grass.[15]

Some of Cen Shen's post-An Lushan rebellion poems combine the themes of battle and nature. The result is sometimes works of exceptional pointedness wherein both conventions are invigorated. Of this group, his most successful effort is Poem 31, which will be discussed in the section on nostalgia. The following poem is addressed to a neighbor near Yanshi, Henan:

20. On Passing Mr. Wang's Retreat At Black Rock Valley, Mt. Gou
Pentasyllabic ancient style

Your former abode was below Mt. Gou;
You got to know the clouds of Mt. Gou.
The retired gentleman has not returned for
  so long;
Seeing the clouds is like seeing you.
Ten autumns have passed since we parted.
Arms and horses, each day so tumultuous.
At Green Creek they made a battlefield;
In Black Valley they posted marching soldiers.
Then they ordered the likes of Chao and You;
They chased afar the herds of deer and elk.
There's only the waters of South Torrent,
Trickling and rippling as of old.[16] (2039)

Contemplations of the Past

Cen Shen was described by Du Que as having been widely read in the histories. Like most scholar-officials he saw the past as both a mirror and a foil to the present. The rise and fall of dynasties were viewed as cyclical phenomena; in this sense historical events elucidate the affairs of the present. On the other hand, the progression of dynasties was perceived as one of deterioration; hence the golden age of the past furnishes a contrast to the degenerate present.

The Poems　　　　　　　　　　　　　　　　　　　　　　　　　　31

Both attitudes make history relevant to contemporary affairs. As a poetic theme, therefore, history has enduring appeal in China.[17]

The following quatrain is one of Cen's early compositions:

21. Spring Affairs in the Mountain Abode
Heptasyllabic quatrain. Date: ca. 742

Liang Gardens at sunset, crows fly wildly.
A desolate horizon and a few homesteads.
Trees in the courtyard, not knowing the men
　are all gone,
At spring put forth the flowers of yester-years.
(2106)

Liang Gardens was built by Liu Wu, Prince of Liang, near Shangqiu, Henan. Liu Wu was a magnanimous patron and the benefactor of many literati including Sima Xiangru (170-117 B.C.) and Mei Sheng (d. 140 B.C.).[18] He is frequently remembered by later literati who were frustrated in their search for a generous and understanding patron.

In this well-turned quatrain, the young Cen Shen dutifully abides by the conventions of historical poems. The composition is divided into a couplet about the present desolation and another which suggests past splendor. The implicit contrast between the finality of human death and nature's power for regeneration is familiar to poetic contemplations of the past, as is the denial of sentience to the flowering trees. In the main, this quatrain is a competent if unexceptional example of Cen's early poetry composed at a time when he was still complying without resistance to standard poetic practice.

The next piece, most likely another early work, was inspired by the *fu* "Changmen" by Sima Xiangru, a composition written at the behest of the imperial consort A Jiao[19] to win back the Emperor Wu of Han, who was angered by her inordinate jealousy and banished her to Changmen Palace:

22. The Plaint of Changmen
Pentasyllabic regulated style

My lord, offended by my jealousy,
Incarcerated me within Changmen.
Dancing sleeves drape from a new love;

Sorrowing brows knit on an old favorite.
Green coin lichens encroach my
  footprints;
Rouge powder wet with tear streaks.
Shamed by a young peach's disdain,
Mute and alone I look at the spring.
(2064)

In both sentiment and diction the poem shows the unmistakable impress of the palace style that was rapidly becoming unfashionable during Cen's young manhood. Typical of that style are the exquisite sentiments matched by preciosity of expression and by self-conscious, precisely balanced couplets. As in the last piece, stock expressions yield a stock response.

More redolent of the vigorous style of the High Tang[20] and much less shackled by existing conventions is a late quatrain composed during the poet's tour of duty at Guozhou in farewell to a friend:

23. Escorting Administrative Officer Liu to Jin and Jiang from the Back Pavilion of Guozhou
Heptasyllabic quatrain. Date: 759-61

The road to the western plains dangles from
  the citadel.
Guests disperse from the red pavilion before
  the rain has stopped.
When you leave, Sir, see if over the Fen waters,
The white clouds are still like those of that
  Han autumn. (2104)

This is a parting poem dedicated to a friend leaving Guozhou for the region that is now Linfen and Jiang, Shanxi. The farewell is said with a reference to an historical incident; the River Fen is the place where the famous Emperor Wu of the Han dynasty had composed a lament for his lost youth and faltering prowess. Cen's last line alludes to his "Autumn Song," which contains the lines: "The autumn wind rises, white clouds fly; / Grass withers, wild geese return south."[21] The quatrain has several features typical of Cen's mature style. He is frequently praised for initial lines that are as vigorous as they are startling; in this poem the reader is surprised by both the appropriateness and newness of the

verb "dangle" (gua) to describe the precipitous road leading
from the citadel on high. The bold tone of this beginning
line is sustained by the allusion to the heroic Emperor Wu.
On the surface the reference seems to be a casual inquiry to
a traveler visiting a locale associated with a famous
historical figure. On the deeper level, it evokes the sense,
so pervasive in poetic contemplations of the past, of life's
brevity and death's finality. The consolation traditionally
proffered to the traveler in parting poetry acquires new
insight when it is presented in conjunction with this
awareness of the inherent instability of human affairs.
Against the backdrop of mutability, the pangs of separation
can only appear inconsequential. Solace is thus achieved by
placing the present change within the panorama of historical
flux. The skillful intermingling of discrete poetic
conventions, in this case those of parting and of history, is
characteristic of Cen's mature style.

Cen Shen adopts the conventions of the poems on history
in another farewell composition which was inspired by the
Han folk song "Mulberry by the Path"; the early poem
recounts how the virtuous maiden Qin Lofu resisted the
advances of a dissolute envoy:[22]

24. The Song of the Fu Waters:[23] Upon Escorting Dou Jian to the Capital
Heptasyllabic ancient style

Lofu of yore was a daughter of the Qin house.
She has been gone for a thousand years, void
 is her home.
The waters that flowed of yore flow yet today;
A myriad affairs chased by their easterly flow.
Those waters flow easterly to the end of time,
With a sound like the waters of former days.
Flowers by the shore still blush for her pink
 blooming face;
Willows upon the bank copy her kingfisher brows.
Spring goes and autumn comes, never waiting;
The moon's hues in the water, forever
 unchanging.
Those silkworms reared by Lofu, empty to our ear;
The five steeds of the envoy, where are they
 today?
In the frosty sky of the ninth month, just as the
 waters chill;

My friend leaves for the west, astride his saddle.
Haply, in the depth of the river are countless carp;
After you leave I'd like you to drop a line. (2051)

Lines 11 and 12 echo three lines of the Han poem: "Lofu likes mulberries and silkworms"; and "The envoy comes from the north, / His five horses shilly and shally." Cen's theme, however, is wholly original. Water, which is not evoked in the earlier poem, serves as a vehicle for several tenors: as a means of transportation, it tacitly refers to the departing friend, and as a symbol of time's relentless passage, it is one of the standard tropes of poetic contemplations of the past; the current of the Fu River as a marker for time thus underlines the elegiac statement of the Han maiden's demise. After developing the two stock connotations of water, Cen proceeds to link it to another trope in an association at once witty and novel. The carp of the penultimate line refers to the real fishes of the Fu; in poetry "double carp" is also a kenning for letters sent from afar.[24] Hence, the poem concludes with a request to his departing friend to write and keep in touch. In the locus classicus of the trope, another Han ballad entitled "Watering My Horse at the Cavern Below the Great Wall," the carp letter is used in a catachresis: "I call my page to cook the carp, / Within is a letter writ in silk."[25] Readers familiar with the Han poem will notice Cen's ingenuity in inventing a catachresis of his own; when he enjoins his friend to "drop a line," he places the carp letter in the river rather than in the kitchen.

Carpe Diem

Like the last group, this body of poems is based upon the realization of the brevity of life and the finality of death. The realization is made in personal rather than historical terms and the resolution is to seize what each day offers. The following two poems are among the most unusual of Cen's works:

25. Song: The Flowering Tree of Assistant Secretary Wei's Home
Heptasyllabic ancient style.
Date: ca. 765[26]

The flowers this year are lovely as last year;

> The man since last year is older this year.
> Know then, an aging man cannot match the flowers;
> Pity the fallen flowers, do not sweep them away.
>
> You and your brothers cannot be rivaled;
> A minister, a censor, and a secretary in the
>   State Department.
> You return from court, under the flowers you often
>   regale your guests.
> Flowers flutter towards the jade vat with spring
>   wine so fragrant. (2058)

Lines 5 and 6 allude to two lines in "Meeting in a Narrow Road," a Han poem which celebrates the splendor and concord of a thriving family: "Older and younger brothers, two or three, / The middle one is vice president of a ministry."[27] The title itself is inspired by another line from the Han poem "Within the courtyard grows a cassia tree."

The composition of this poem is daring; the piece may be divided into two tetrastichs that contrast with each other in sentiment, rhetoric, and rhyme. The first four lines make a general statement about human inconstancy, whereas the second set of four lines attends to a specific occasion that represents convivality. The rhyme in the first tetrastich falls on words in the oblique <u>hao</u> rhyming category while in the second tetrastich, the rhyme belongs to the level toned <u>yang</u> category. Words in the level tone are sometimes described in traditional poetics as sonorous and pleasing, while the oblique and entering tones are considered sharp and shrill. The polar attitudes of sadness and joy coalesce in the image of the flowering trees of the first and concluding lines.

The first four lines attend to life's inherent sadness with exquisite tact. After stating that man, lacking nature's ability to renew itself, is less fortunate than the flowering tree, the poem proceeds to lament the sad fate of the flowers. The poignancy of the human condition is the more rueful for being unexpressed. The second tetrastich addresses itself to life's joy in a multi-faceted statement. It extols the pleasure of friendship in a statement that contains a covert reference to a poem that celebrates familial concord and fraternal amity. Thus the lines evoke all that the traditional Chinese cherishes and values in life.

Cen Shen uses the motif of the flower again in another poem whose middle lines, in the <u>Complete Tang Poetry</u>

version, repeat two lines of the last poem:

26. Song: The Hollyhock
Irregular ancient style

Yesterday a flower in bloom,
Today another flower in bloom.
Today's flower at its prime.
Yesterday's flower fast fading.
Know then an aging man cannot match
  the flower.
Pity the fallen flowers, do not sweep
  them away.
In life there is no eternal youth.
Do not stint the wine coins by your bed.
Head for the tavern when you can.
Don't you see, Sir, the hollyhock? (2062)

The poem contains lines of five (lines 1-4 and 9-10) and seven (lines 5-8) syllables. It concludes most unexpectedly, for the poetic formula "don't you see, Sir?" (jun bujian), a common exclamation in folk and literary ballads, customarily opens a poem or introduces a sustained description. As the formula is identified with poetic opening rather than closure, this poem seems to end in mid-statement. Its meaning, in fact, is complete, but the impression of a truncated conclusion reinforces the statement that life can be cut short most abruptly.

Nostalgia

The themes of the soldier forced to leave his home on long campaigns and of the woman he left behind are as old as Chinese poetry itself, for they appear in the Shijing (Book of Songs). In later poetry the theme of nostalgia is expanded to include such expressions as those of the literati-official delegated or exiled to remote regions and the plaint of the merchant's wife abandoned by a peripatetic husband. In the course of a life filled with much travel Cen Shen had many occasions to express his longing for his home. Some of these compositions are among the most popular pieces he wrote.

So strong is the traditional Chinese attachment to home, and so unequivocal his loathness to leave it, poems of nostalgia have an appeal that is unparalleled by other poetic themes. Home-longing, perhaps, furnished the subject for more popular songs than romantic love itself. The attachment to home is as absolute as it is uncomplicated. Neither discord nor opposite viewpoint exists in a loyalty that is at once singleminded and simple. The poet's task in the poetry of nostalgia is not to achieve that "balance or reconcilation of opposite or discordant qualities," which Coleridge asks for, or to forge an unformed consciousness, but to renew a familiar one. He must find the perfect image or moment to revive an overripe sentiment. This Cen was able to do with varying degrees of success in the following quatrains:

27. Meeting an Envoy Going to the Capital
Heptasyllabic quatrain

Looking east to the garden of my home, a road
  without end.
The twin sleeves of a decrepit man, tear
  stained and not dry.
We meet on horseback, there is no brush nor
  paper;
I'll just count on you to pass the word that
  I'm well. (2106)

28. Sent to Registrar Li of Chang'an from Jade Pass[28]

Chang'an to the east is a myriad miles and more;
My friend, you'll surely drop me a note.
Looking westwards from Jade Pass can break one's
  heart,
Especially when tomorrow morning is New Year's
  Eve. (2104)

29. Passing Weizhou in the West, I See the Wei Waters and Think of the Land of Qin
Pentasyllabic quatrain

The waters of the Wei flow eastwards;
When will they reach Yongzhou?
I add to them two rows of tears,
To send to the gardens of my home.[29]
(2102)

30. Sent to My Family from Lucerne Beacon
Heptasyllabic quatrain

Beside Lucerne Beacon I meet spring arriving;
At Gourd River tears wet my lapel.
Within the boudoir, vain longings;
No sight of the battlefield man, whelmed by gloom.[30] (2104)

31. Moving with the Army on the Ninth Day, I Think of My Gardens in Chang'an
Pentasyllabic quatrain. Date: ca. 757

Most strongly do I wish to scale the heights;
No one comes with wine.
Far away, I pity the chrysanthemums of my garden,
Blooming by the battlefield. (2103)

The last piece is by far the boldest and most admired of the five quatrains. The Double Ninth, or the ninth day of the ninth month, was traditionally a day for family reunion. Custom called for climbing to a high place to compose poetry and to drink wine. Since the chrysanthemum belongs to the autumn, it became a tradition to drink wine made from the flower petals; and because "nine" (jiu) is a homonym of "perpetual," the day is also associated with longevity. The Double Ninth in poetry is associated with Tao Qian, whose several compositions commemorating this day are constantly echoed by later poets. Thus the reference to absence of wine in line 2 of Cen's piece is an allusion to Tao's "The Double Ninth in Retirement," where he claims that he has "no way to come by wine."[31]

Cen Shen yokes the Double Ninth motif with its traditional eremitic associations to the theme of war to stunning effect. Composed during the An Lushan occupation of Chang'an, it is a forceful statement about the topsy-turvy world. The transference of the Double Ninth setting to the battlefield is a bold poetic strategy that makes a more pointed statement than Du Fu's "The Moon Rising," which also describes a war-torn garden:

> The myriad states still repel the rebels.
> What is my garden like?
> Returning I find few familiar things;
> It has long since become many battlefields. (2518)

Among the poems of nostalgia in the longer verse forms, the two following pieces have gained considerable attention in traditional Chinese poetics:

32. Journeying in the Mountains in Late Autumn
Pentasyllabic ancient style

A weary horse crouches on the long slope;
The evening sun sets over the ford.
A mountain wind blows into the empty wood,
Swish-swishing as if someone were here.
Gris-green fall sky clears from a cool wind.
Rocky road without flying dust.
A thousand thoughts gather at this dusk season;
A myriad strains sorrow for the autumnal morn.
The goatsucker last evening called;
The orchid's hues already faded.
What's more, the man on a long journey,
Naturally has much toil. (2045)

Yin Fan (ca. 753), the Tang compiler of the Heyue yingling ji, singles out the second couplet of this poem as being "the essence of reclusion."[32] Scholars after him continue to acknowledge the lines as a perfect example also of the "desolation of a long journey."[33] Such remarks are confined to a single, felicitous couplet and take no account of the integrality of the composition.

With feelings too strong to be explicitly stated, the poet allows the sequestered setting to register his sense of isolation and the autumnal season as well as the dying day to express his weariness and regret for time lost. The "myriad sounds" externalize his countless and chaotic thoughts just as the goatsucker's cries render his own muteness more poignant. The faded orchid, the flower associated with virtue since the "Lisao," embodies his own decline. Cen realizes the perfect correlation between external object and internal emotion. Following the imagistic, high style of the first ten lines - expressions such as xiaochen ("autumnal morn"), wanli ("myriad strain"), and cangming ("gris-green fall sky") belong to poetic diction - the final and only overt statement of hardship with its colloquial kuangzai ("what's more") and ziran ("naturally") seems anticlimactic and prosaic.

33. A Night Letter from a Boat in Banan
Pentasyllabic regulated style.
Date: 766 or later

At the ferry it is almost dusk;
Home farers vie to cross, clamoring.
A bell nearby clarifies a rustic stupa;
A fire far off lights a river hamlet.
Seeing the wild geese, I think of a letter
 from home.
Hearing the gibbon my eyes well with tear
 streaks.
In a solitary boat ten thousand miles away,
I cannot bear to speak of the autumn moon.
(2091)

Like the previous piece, this poem contains one couplet that has been singled out for comment by Chinese scholars. Hu Zi (ca. 1147) compares the first couplet to the celebrated first lines of Meng Haoran's "Returning to Deer Gate Monastery by Night," and favors Cen's lines as being "more simple and conclusive."[34] Cen draws freely from the common stock of poetic images: the lonely boat, the wild geese associated with letter-bearing, the gibbon of Ba Gorge, and the autumn moon have appeared in countless poems. Yet he also deviates from the marked track of poetic language; line 3 manages to make darkness vivid with the verbal use of the adjectival qing ("clear") as the pivotal third word (known in Chinese poetics as the "eye" of the pentasyllabic line).

Our last three examples use one of Cen's favorite motifs: the homing dream of a traveler far from home.

34. Spending the Night at the West Hostelry of Iron Pass[35]
Pentasyllabic regulated style

The sweat of horses trampled to mud;
In the morning thousands of hooves gallop.
Amidst snow we journey to the corner of the
 earth.
In fiery places we sleep at the sky's tip.
The frontier so far, hearts often terrified.
Our home so distant, dreams too go astray.

Would you know that the moon over the garden
  of my home,
Also comes to shine upon Iron Pass' west?
(2090)

35. Passing Jiuquan I Think of My Villa at Duling
Pentasyllabic regulated style

Last night I slept at Jilian;
This morning I crossed Jiuquan.
To the west, yellow sand ends at the lake;
To the north, white grass joins the sky.
Amidst grief it's hard to pass the day.
My return is still years away.
At Yang Pass, a myriad mile dream
Knows the fields of Duling.[36] (2090)

In these poems, Cen thwarts the normal association of dreams with the reposeful and the passive. Showing the same vigorous and activist attitude that makes his nature poems so distinctive, Cen describes the dreams as forging homeward with the energy of a military march. This disruption of normal associations underscores the abnormality of military life.

The dream motif appears in another poem which depicts the opposite point of view of the wife of the traveler:

36. Spring Dream
Heptasyllabic Quatrain

Last night in the nuptial chamber, the spring
  wind arose.
My love is still sundered by the waters of the
  Xiang.
For a time the spring dream on the pillow,
Traverses the myriad leagues of Jiangnan. (2107)

The Xiang River flows from Guangxi northward through Hunan and ultimately joins Lake Dongting. The locale of the poem in the heartland of China suggests that the lady is the wife of a merchant or an official rather than a soldier. Cen injects a tone of perseverance and indomitablity into this most tender of moments in Chinese poetry when the young bride greets the coming of spring. The languor normally associated with the words "spring dream" is relentlessly negated in the final line, where the dream travels a myriad miles in the quest for the loved one. Cen Shen's poetic signature can often be identified by this wholly new and vigorous interpretation of topoi traditionally associated with fragility and passivity.

Chapter Three
Poetry in a Social Context

The Tang literatus is frequently required to compose verses in response to a variety of social and public occasions. More than a literary accomplishment and a vehicle of personal expression, the art of poetry was also a necessary social skill. The majority of works in the Complete Tang Poetry were written for a specific occasion and fall under such broad categories as: (1) poetic exchanges (chou); (2) poems "presented to" (zeng) and "responding to" (da) certain named individuals; (3) poems composed in "farewell" (songbie) and upon "taking leave" of specific people at departure (liubie); (4) verse sent to absent people (ji). Furthermore, poetry contests and impromptu verse compositions were popular forms of amusement at social gatherings. In court receptions, literary-minded emperors such as Xuanzong would often have his courtiers "accompany" (he) his own compositions with works of their own, or he would hold poetry competitions on designated themes. Verse composed at imperial behest contains the term yingzhi ("responding to royal command") as part of the title. Private parties too included many opportunities to display one's literary wares. Elaborate verse games were devised in the course of the centuries.[1] Many a social gathering was the occasion to compose poems on a given theme or to accompany each other's poems; or else, the literati might take turns composing lines known as "linked verse" (lianju). Rules for such compositions varied with each occasion and the whim of the participants; the requirements ranged from the simple observance of an agreed-upon theme to the involved use of certain words, or the observance of either a specific rhyme word (heshi), a common rhyming category (heyun), or the use of rhymes in the same sequence (ciyun or buyun). The Tang literati might also elect to use a theme with a literary antecedent or the rhyme of an earlier poem (yongyun). As the art of poetry increased in sophistication during the Tang, so the order of difficulty for these exercises grew. The most challenging, the use of rhyme in the same sequence, was not extensively used until the mid-Tang with the exchanges between Yuan Zhen (779-831) and Bo Juyi

(772-846).

Cen Shen is associated with two suites of poems which were composed in the company of contemporary literati and which have gained considerable native critical attention. These are the poems celebrating the morning audience at Daming Palace, which matches works by Jia Zhi, Wang Wei, and Du Fu, and the composition marking an excursion to the Temple of Compassionate Mercy, composed in the company of Du Fu, Gao Shi, Chu Guangxi, and Xue Ju. These two suites provide unique opportunity to compare and discriminate among the skills of several major High Tang poets. Admittedly, the occasion imposed its own formalities; answering to the dictates of protocol and etiquette, these works are hardly the "spontaneous overflow of powerful feelings." They are displays of technical virtuosity that admit no deep inquiry or subtle reasoning. Even so, they are significant, not only because they allow one to observe how gifted poets arrived at different interpretations of, and solutions to, the challenges imposed by a strictly defined form and matter, but also because they illustrate the use of poetry - it is a use that is largely overlooked in contemporary academic discussions of the art - as a medium of game and as an instrument of social communication. We tend to forget sometimes that serious art can also be playful and occasional. The two groups of poems which follow remind us that poetry as game is as disciplined and exacting as the more serious manifestations of the art.

The Morning Audience at Daming Palace

The compositions on the morning audience at Daming Palace were written in the late spring of 758, some months after Suzong's triumphant return to Chang'an following the recapture of the capital from the An Lushan rebels. Wang Wei and Jia Zhi as secretaries of the Grand Imperial Secretariat, and Du Fu and Cen Shen as Reminder and Omissioner, respectively, must have met one another every morning at the Daming Palace, which Suzong had chosen as his quarters.[2] One morning, Jia Zhi, who had inherited the post of supervising the drafting of imperial documents which his father, Jia Ceng, had once held,[3] composed a heptasyllabic regulated style poem:

The Morning Audience at Daming Palace, Presented to Friends and Colleagues of The Two Ministeries

Silver candle to the morning audience, the purple
  road is long.
Spring hues of the Forbidden Quarters, gris-green
  at dawn.
A thousand twigs of frail willows droop before blue
  scrollworks;
A hundred calls from flitting bush warblers fill
  Jianzhang Palace.
Sound of swords and pendants attends the jade court
  yard footsteps;
Attire of caps and robes teased by the royal
  censers' fragrance.
Together we bathe in the gracious waves of Phoenix
  Pond;
Morning after morning, moistening my brush, I wait
  upon my lord.[4] (2596)

Jia Zhi then invited his colleagues and three of the most distinguished poets of the age to compose accompanying poems. They each obliged with a poem in the same verse form.

In Accompaniment to Grand Secretary Jia Zhi's Poem on the Morning Audience at Daming Place
  by Wang Wei

The crimson capped Keeper of the Cock presents the
  dawn tally;
The Lord of the Robes brings forth the kingfisher-
  cloud furs.
Ninefold gates open to palace and council chambers;
Caps and robes from a myriad states bow to the
  jeweled crown.
The sun's color just now, looks down upon the
  immortal palms, stirring;
Fragrant mist about to flank the dragon hem,
  drifting.
The morning audience over, you must supervise the
  variegated edicts;
Sound of girdle pendants return to the end of

Phoenix Pond.[5] (1298)

by Du Fu

The clepsydra at the fifth watch urges the arrows
of dawn.
Spring hues within the ninefold gates intoxicate the
immortal peaches.
Upon banners warmed by the sun, dragons and serpents
stir;
The breeze weakens beside palace chambers, swallows
and martins soar.
The audience over, a fragrant mist leads our sleeves;
The poem completed, jade and pearl at the stroke of a
brush.
If you want to know the father's edicts, so beautiful,
Upon the pond today, there's another phoenix feather.
(2410)

37. by Cen Shen

A cock crows on the purple road, chilly the dawn light;
Bush warblers sing in the royal domain, tardy the hues
of spring.
With the morning bells from metallic gates, a myriad
doors open;
Towards the imperial insignia on the jade steps, a
thousand courtiers surge.
Blossoms greet our swords and pendants as the stars
first set;
Willows brush the flags and pennons when the dew
is not yet dry.
Alone at Phoenix Pond, there is a guest,
Whose "Song of Bright Spring" is hard to match.[6]
(2096)

    This suite of poems is widely represented in anthologies of Tang poetry for both historical and literary interests. Composed shortly after the reinstatement of the Tang house to the throne, the morning audience heralds more than a new day in court; it symbolizes the hopes for a new period of stability and prosperity under the restored monarchy. From the point of view of literary history, the poems mark a milestone in the development of classical poetry. It has been observed that the longer regulated form did not become fully developed until after the An Lushan rebellion. The form is all but unrepresented in the works of the great poets who flourished in the kaiyuan era, such as Meng Haoran and Li Bo, and is used by Du Fu almost solely in the poems that date to 757 and beyond. The four poems on the morning audience at Daming Palace are among the earliest mature examples of the heptasyllabic regulated style.[7] For these reasons and also because some of the greatest names of Tang poetry are associated with it, this cycle of poems has engaged considerable attention in native treatises of poetry.

In the main, native literary scholars have been occupied by discussions of the relative merits of the four poems; Xie Zhen (1495-1575) recounts an occasion when he and several companions tried to rank the four pieces but failed to come to any agreement.[8] Li Rihua (1565-1635) singles out the most successful couplet from each piece as a means of discerning their relative merits.[9] Modern readers may find such evaluations unconvincing. Their appreciation of the poems may, perhaps, be better served with a consideration of the requirements and problems attendant upon the making of the poetry of accompaniment, as well as each individual work's solution to the demands of such verses.

No attempt is made to match rhyme in this suite, the burden of merit falling wholly on the poet's skill in treating the given theme of the morning audience. Connoisseurs of classical poetry look for scrupulous adherence to the theme and would consider inappropriate digression as an error of judgment and lack of skill. The theme in question is a courtly one and as such, precludes any treatment other than the most dignified and reverent. The great Song poet Yang Wanli (1127-1206) defines the requisite tone as "refined and of sufficient magnitude,"[10] whereas Weng Fanggang (1733-1818) demands that it be both "vigorous and beautiful."[11] Yang Zai (1271-1323) claims that works on courtly themes should be "sumptuous and dignified, refined and polished."[12] Beyond the strictures imposed by the theme, the accompanying pieces by Du Fu, Wang Wei, and Cen Shen are expected to respond in many artful ways to the opening poem. Traditional treatises often compare the poetry of accompaniment to a bell; it echoes and reverberates with the sound and sense of the companion piece, thus creating many lingering afterthoughts. Should the beginning diverge from the matching poem, then the conclusion should ideally converge. Stated another way, a poem of accompaniment must make its own unique and independent statement on a shared theme while acknowledging and evoking its complementary piece in many ingenious ways. The poet is expected to create variation within the same context, to achieve a balance of dissonance and consonance.

These considerations are apparent in the present cycle. All four pieces conclude on a note of monophonal accord in the reference to Phoenix Pond which contains a tribute to Jia Zhi, the leader of this verse game. Jia himself had ended his poem with the deft words of a courtier avowing loyalty to his sovereign. Wang Wei speaks of his official duties with the reference to the variegated edicts, while Cen Shen compliments him on his poem, rare as the "Song of Sunny Spring." Du Fu's tribute is the most ingenious of all. His concluding couplet lauds both Jia Zhi and his father with a witty play on the name "Phoenix Pond"; for "Phoenix feather" is a trope for the worthy scion of a worthy father. All four poems thus converge at the conclusion. The earlier couplets, however, are an intricate dance of converging and diverging movements. They fork in the first line, which evokes dawn at different places, only to join at the image of the palace gate (line 2 in Jia and Du Fu, line 3 in Cen and Wang). Couplets 2 and 3 make different configurations of a number of shared images. The reader will find many correspondences within these lines too obvious to require commentary.

Traditional scholars consistently point out that the "accompaniment" in this cycle takes place only on the thematic level and that no attempt was made to match rhyme.[13] It is unlikely, however, that the sensitive responses to the sense of Jia Zhi's poem are not complimented in some way by acknowledgment of its sound. The deviations (ao) from tonic regularity in the three accompanying poems seem to respond to Jia's composition also. Jia's poem contains the following deviations:[14] (1) the first word of each of the first three lines departs from tonic regularity. These are free positions which do not require, though they often receive, compensation (jiu), that is, changing the tone in another position in either the same line or the matching line in the interest of maintaining tonic contrast and balance. (2) Line 6 begins with three level tones, qieu ("robe"), guan ("cap"), shin ("body")[15] as a result of a deviation in the third word. Such a sequence of level tones is deemed to have an ancient flavor, an effect deliberately cultivated in some regulated verse to achieve variation. (3) The sixth word of lines 5 and 7, djhi ("step"), djhui ("pond") also deviates from the rule and is compensated by the fifth word, ngiok ("jade"), bhiung ("phoenix"). Since the even-numbered positions in each line generally cannot entertain deviation, the modern linguist Wang Li terms this pattern a "special deviation" (te'ao),[16] and he observes that it enjoyed a vogue among Tang poets.

Of the three types of deviations present in Jia Zhi's poem, the last two are the most significant since the first takes place in what is generally acknowledged as a free tonic position. The fact that the second and third deviations are echoed in the poems accompanying Jia's may not be fortuitous. Wang Wei might be responding to Jia's third deviation, for his most pronounced departure from tonic pattern occurs in the fifth word, ngo ("five") of line 7 and results in a line that ends with three words in the oblique tone. Du Fu begins his sixth line with three words in the level tone, shi ("poem"), zhiaeng ("complete"), jio ("pearl"), thus reproducing the deviation of Jia's counterpart line. Among the three accompanying poems, Cen Shen's is the most regular in terms of tonic pattern. Yet a significant and uncompensated deviation in his composition, the third word of line 7, bhiung ("phoenix"), is again one which Jia Zhi had rendered tonically deviant. In fact, the words "phoenix" and "pond" are made tonically irregular in three of the four poems (the exception is Wang Wei's poem). Tonic deviation, of course, serves a euphonic purpose by breaking up the monotony of established patterns. From the point of view of meaning, it may accentuate a particularly significant word or passage. The cluster of deviations at "phoenix" or "pond" suggests that sound and sense are correlated here, while other departures from tonic regularity may indicate that the effort to accompany Jia Zhi was made on the acoustic as well as the thematic levels.

Having considered the poems as segments of one complete suite, it behooves us now to examine each piece as a self-contained statement. Jia Zhi's opening poem is ordered around the perspective of the courtier, for it commences with his departure for the palace before daybreak. The first three lines are suffused in color and light that move from night in the image of the silver candle to the misty half-light of "gris-green," and then to daylight and the clearly defined color of blue scrollwork behind the willow trees. The next three lines then appeal to the auditory and olfactory senses with the morning call of the bush warblers (line 4), the silence of the palace courtyard broken by the clank of swords and pendants, and finally the incense that "teases the official robes." The concluding couplet is correct and dignified.

Wang Wei's piece is a kaleidoscope of colors ranging from the brilliant contrast between the crimson cap and the kingfisher furs of the first couplet to the shimmer of sunlight playing upon the dew in the third. The spectrum coalesces in the variegated edicts of the penultimate line. Color words qualify the sartorial images which appear in five of the eight lines and which confer imagistic coherence to the poem. Wang exercises considerable ingenuity in matching Jia's poem. Jia had elected to present his description from the point of view of the courtier leaving his home by candlelight. Wang Wei achieves similitude in dissimilitude by anchoring his perspective within the palace. The first couplet presents the emperor awakening to the call of the Keeper of the Cock and then, shortly afterwards, dressed in his formal robes. On the other hand, Wang is equally careful not to disrupt the continuity with Jia completely; "Ninefold gates open to palace and council chambers" (line 3) is a natural sequel to Jia's second line: "Spring hues of the Forbidden Quarters, gris-green at dawn." The burden to match Jia might have weakened the line, for Shi Buhua (1836-1890) feels that Wang's third line is constrictive and pedestrian.[17] The next lines describe the audience and continue the interplay of divergence from and convergence with the opening poem. Whereas Jia had invited his reader to witness the ceremony from the ranks of the courtiers, Wang presents the same scene, but from the vantage point of the throne. Like the sun hovering over the palace statuary, the sovereign "looks down" upon his subjects. Instead of "teasing" the courtiers' attire as in Jia Zhi, the incense flanks the hem of the imperial robe like attendants. The last line concludes the poem on a note of lingering resonance, with the sound of girdle pendants growing ever fainter as it fades to the far end of Phoenix Pond. Chinese taste tends to favor an evocative to a defined closure.

Du Fu's treatment of the court audience differs radically from those of his companions. His second couplet is universally admired. Li Rihua[18] praises the antithesis between the emblematic dragon and the real birds, as well as the verve of the verbs "stir" and "soar." The reference to the birds also evokes an ancient proverb: "Swallows and martins rejoice when the great mansion is completed." The saying represents man's need for a strong and stable society in the birds' search for the safe eaves of a well-built house. Unlike the other three poets, Du Fu pointedly refrains from describing the court ceremony. The first four lines depict the palace from a distance and, in a significant departure from the procedure of the companion pieces, Du Fu omits any reference to the human participants of the ceremony. By line 5 he has stated that the audience is dismissed and he proceeds to address his companions directly and to pay his elegant compliment to Jia Zhi. His is an outsider's view of the morning audience, and as such it is criticized by Lu Shiyong[19] (1089-1153) for failing to adhere to the designated theme. Lu also objects to the expression "intoxicating peaches" as a lapse from decorum. Other scholars, however, have suggested that the poet deliberately establishes a distance between himself and the court to express his sense of alienation from it. Like many of Du Fu's works, this poem has been submitted to an allegorical reading; lines 3 to 6 have been read as an indictment of Suzong's court, with the faint breeze representing the atmosphere of moral weakness and the high flying, small birds, a symbol of the mean-spirited men who held important positions in that court. Such interpretations remain, perforce, at the level of the conjectural; yet it is hard to dispute the fact that Du's presentation lacks the grandeur and opulence of his companion pieces. A reason for his failure to achieve such an effect may be the unresolved conflict between the impulse to express intensely personal feelings and the obligation to utter the correct public sentiment. As paean and as poem of accompaniment, Du's composition is certainly more problematic than the other poems.

Like Wang Wei's and unlike Du Fu's version, Cen Shen's composition on the "Morning Audience at Daming Palace" is marked by consummate artistry undistracted by deep or disturbing thoughts. In keeping with the formality of the theme, balance and symmetry characterize Cen's poem. The first line of the initial couplet refers to "chilly dawn," and the second line speaks of "tardy spring"; the subject of the dawn is then amplified in the second couplet and that of spring in the third pair of lines. With the exception of the first and concluding lines, each of the other six lines contain at least one image already evoked by Jia Zhi. Cen thus redeems more of Jia's original imagery than either Du Fu or Wang Wei. In this sense, it is the most diligent effort to accompany Jia Zhi.

Whereas Jia Zhi and Wang Wei had begun their poems by viewing the activities of courtier and sovereign, respectively, Cen presents an objective description with no apparent human presence. Although the device is not required at this point, some regulated poems elect to use parallelism in the first couplet. In an interesting variation on this optional parallelism, Cen's initial couplet achieves phonic but not semantic antithesis. A word-for-word translation yields.

```
cock        crow        purple  road    dawn    light   chilly
bush warbler sing       royal   domain  spring  color   tardy
```

Each character in the second line finds a semantic and grammatical match in the counterpart position of the first line with the exception of the third word: "royal" (yiwang) does not belong to the same semantic category as "purple," but one of its homonyms is "yellow," a color word that is an acceptable antithesis for "purple." Chou Zhao'ao (1638-1717) calls this verbal device "false parallelism," while Wang Li terms it "sound loan."[20]

Cen evokes correspondences between the human and natural world to create a sense of cosmic harmony. Beginning with the call of the cock and the song of the bush warbler, the poem concludes with a human song. Human artifacts wrought in jade and gold compliment the natural exquisiteness of flowers and willows. The burnished metal of the great palace gates reflects the glitter of the stars just as the chill of white jade stairs is repeated in the cold of the white dew. The communion of natural splendor and human opulence becomes complete in the justly celebrated third couplet where day and night, court and nature merge into each other in lines of fluid elegance. The vision is one of universal concord.

Typical of many of Cen's poems, this composition seems to move at an urgent pace, first established by the word "tardy" in line two. Two strong verbs of motion follow, the expansive "open" and the constrictive "surge." The next couplet depicts time in process, the brief instant when "stars first fall" and "the dew is not yet dried." At least one native critic has questioned the appropriateness of the brisk pace; Hu Yinglin (1551-1603) feels that a stately theme calls for a more measured movement and that the second couplet especially is unduly precipitate.[21] Cen's concluding couplet is elegant although lacking the cunning of Du Fu's compliment to Jia Zhi.

The Poems on the Stupa of the Temple of Compassionate Mercy

Cen Shen was also part of the making of another cycle of poems when he visited the Buddhist Temple of Compassionate Mercy with Gao Shi, Xue Ju, Du Fu, and Chu Guangxi.

The temple was one of the wonders of Tang dynasty Chang'an. Located in the Jinye Quarters west of Vermilion Bird Gate, it was built on the site of an old Sui dynasty temple. In 646, when he was still the Crown Prince, Gaozong dedicated it to his mother, the Wende Empress. The temple sat on some of Chang'an's choicest land; its southern grounds looked out to the imperial canal and boasted of a bamboo grove that was unrivaled in the western capital. But it was its western side with the six-tiered stupa, soaring to some three hundred Chinese feet, that was celebrated in antiquity. The structure was first built in 652 in the style of the "tumulus of the western regions." Some fifty years later, in the Chang'an era (701-705), it was rebuilt on a yet grander scale. With its eastern entrance dignified by stone tablets inscribed with the writings of two Tang emperors, Taizong and Gaozong, and housing a rare collection of sutras, the new stupa was a magnificent affair. Following the reconstruction, it served the court and the denizens of the capital in a variety of ways that had little to do with religious practices. It often received the Tang emperors on pleasure excursions. Triumphant _jinshi_ winners were invited to inscribe their names there.[22]

The pilgrimage which furnished the occasion of these poems took place most probably in the autumn of 752.[23] The procedure for composition seemed to have differed from that of the previous cycle; all four of the extant versions are in the pentasyllabic ancient style, but there does not appear to have been a formally acknowledged opening poem to which the other pieces must respond. Since Gao Shi and Xue Ju alone were named in the title of Cen Shen's poem, and also since a note by Du Fu, placed after the title of his poem, states that Gao's and Xue's poems were already finished, there is some reason to think that they were the hosts on this occasion and hence opened the round of versemaking. Xue Ju's poem is now lost. Gao Shi's is as follows:

Ascending the Stupa of the Temple of Compassionate Mercy with Several Gentlemen

Within the confused crowd there is a fragrant
  region;
A stupa, its aspect of differentiation.
We ascend, awed by the lone height;
Windflapped, we rejoice in the "power of the
  great" edifice.
It is as if we have sprouted wings;
Afar, we go above the void.
For an instant we think our bodies part from
  the world;
Then we feel our form and spirit invigorated.
Palaces and watchtowers all before the door;
Mountains and rivers without exception lean
  towards the eaves.
The autumn wind arrived last evening;
The Qin frontier, yet more clear and wide.
A thousand leagues, how gris-green;
We look upon the Five Mounds, lush and dense.
In this thriving age I blush for Commandant
  Ruan;
Even before taking office, I knew of Zhou Fang.
They are presented as models but there is no
  reason;
Henceforth let me roam with abandon.[24] (2204)

The poem describes the ascent to the top of the stupa and the view from the summit. Yet it is not so much the objective description responsible only to the truth of the outside world as the constituent of a trope which engages the poet's interest. In keeping with the theme, all four poems in this cycle contain a liberal sprinkling of Buddhist terminology. Gao evokes other philosophic texts as well; "fragrant region" and "aspect of differentiation" are Buddhist terms, while the locus classicus of "spirit invigorated" and "windflapped" is the Zhuangzi. In line 4, the stupa is called "power of the great" (dazhuang), the name of one of the hexagrams of the Book of Changes. In brief, the ascent is rendered in a manner that is as much descriptive as it is prefigurative of a serious philosophic journey.

Beginning with the fifth couplet, Gao Shi offers a description of the sweeping view from the summit. He avails himself of two time-honored poetic conventions. First, physical height has long been associated with spiritual elevation in classical poetry. The broad vista atop the stupa brings enlightenment and leads the poet to contemplate the truth of the Buddhist belief in the insubstantiality and ephemerality of worldly attainment. Mortality, that great leveler of worldly degree, is evoked in lines 11-14, where autumn and the five burial mounds of the Han emperors outside Chang'an invite intimations of death. A second, related convention which appears in this poem is that of space as a marker for time. Centuries and distance meet and speak with the same voice. The thousand leagues (line 13) represent the centuries of time which is reinforced by the image of the Five Mounds. In the last four lines, the poet, going back in time, evokes two famous literati of antiquity who might serve as models for his own life: the free-spirited Ruan Ji (210-263), who had accepted a post as commandant of an infantry, because of the fine cellar that went with the office, and the diligent Zhou Fang (28-105), who was appointed to his first office before the age of twenty and went on to write multi-tomed works. Gao, whose unrestrained, knightly (xia) temperament is widely noted in literary history, refuses to emulate both extremes of conduct, for in the final couplet he declares he would henceforth "roam with abandon." This expression had described the great nature poet Xie Lingyun (385-433); when he was forced to accept an official position, Xie had insisted on "roaming in abandon" in the same manner as when he was a private gentleman living on his Yongjia estate. Ultimately, therefore, Gao seems to embrace the ideal of the resilient man who can maintain an untrammeled spirit both within and without officialdom.

We cannot be sure about the order in which the remaining three poems were originally composed, but since Du Fu had mentioned only Gao Shi and Xue Ju as preceding him, it is perhaps appropriate that we consider his poem next:

> Its height straddles the grey sky;
> The piercing wind never ceases.
> Since I do not have an enlightened man's heart;
> Climbing it perversely brings a hundred cares.
> Only now do I know that the power of the teaching by symbols

Is worthy of pursuit in depth.
Overhead, we thread through the caverns of
  dragons and serpents;
First we emerge from the gloom of beams
  and spans.
The seven stars are at the Dipper;
The sound of the Heavenly River flows
  westwards.
Xi He, the charioteer, whips the white sun;
Shao Hao moves the clear autumn.
The Qin mountain suddenly shatters;
The waters of Jing and Wei cannot be found.
Looking down, only the air;
How can one discern the royal domain?
Turning my head I call for Shun.
The clouds over his grave are sorrowing.
Alas for the revel at Jasper Pond,
As the sun sets over Mt. Kunlun.
The yellow swan leaves and does not stop,
With plaintive cries, where will it go?
Look at the geese following the sun,
Each with its own plan for millet and
  rice.^{25} (2258)

The poem carries a heavy freight of mythological references apparently unrelated to the theme of the pilgrimage to a Buddhist shrine. Lines 11 and 12 allude to two dieties, Xi He, the charioteer of the sun, and Shao Hao, the god of autumn. Lines 17 and 18 refer to the sage-king Shun and to his burial at Cangwu, attended by his two devoted consorts. Jasper Pond is the locale of the banquet which the Queen Mother of the West held in honor of King Mu of Zhou.

Because of Du Fu's preeminent place in Chinese poetry and because some of his most vigorous poetic statements were inspired by contemporary affairs, traditional commentators have proposed allegorical interpretations for a number of his works. The mythological allusions of this poem are sometimes submitted to such a reading. The legend of the Queen Mother of the West feting King Mu is read as having a contemporary counterpart in the dalliance of Xuanzong with the Lady Yang at another celebrated body of waters, the Hot Spring at the foot of Mt. Li. Qian Qianyi (1582-1664) suggests that Shun represents Taizong, whose exemplary conduct in dedicating the stupa to his consort-mother is in striking contrast to his descendant's license with his concubine.²⁶ The blurred vista (lines 13-16) is seen as representing the moral confusion of the day when right and wrong, figured in the clear waters of the Jing and the turbid Wei, are no longer distinguishable. The yellow swan and the geese which conclude the poem are interpreted as marking two types of men: those who are like the mythical swan and flee the world of compromise to uncertain destination; and those others, like the wild geese following the sun, who serve a benighted emperor out of self-interest. The allegorical reading offers a possible resolution to the puzzling mythological references; yet it leaves the reader without any clearer perception of the poem's aesthetic and affective powers.

The view from the summit in Du Fu's composition differs markedly from that of Gao Shi. Instead of a clear vista, Du finds a beclouded sky that obstructs his vision. Du seems to be subverting the sacrosanct poetic convention whereby physical ascent is associated with spiritual elevation and poetic inspiration. The topoi of the extended perspective, afforded by the vantage point of a mountain or a high building, leading to both philosophical enlightenment as well as heightened powers of expressing this state, goes as far back as the Hanshi waizhuan (Exoteric commentary on the Han text of the Shijing), in the second century B.C. It appears in Wang Can's (177-217) fu "On Ascending the Tall Building," which states that "climbing this building and scanning the four directions dispel sorrows."²⁷ Du Fu deliberately reverses this convention when he avers that climbing the stupa "perversely brings a hundred worries."

The ascent up the stupa is presented as a journey to some mythological realm; the dark stairwell leading to the top is "the cavern of dragons and serpents," while at the summit the autumn sky is evoked through two dieties. Contrary to expectations, physical elevation does not bring exhilaration. Du Fu's initial heavy mood is not dispelled, for the height fails to yield that clear vista that the experienced reader of Chinese poetry expects. His vision of space blocked by the thick mist, the poet tries to move back in time by considering the mythological past of Shun and the Queen Mother of the West; he is equally disappointed, for Cangwu too is shrouded in clouds and Jasper Pond is irretrievably lost to man. Stalled in his search in both space and time, the poem ends with two avian images that promise freedom and release. The poet's stultification might well have stemmed from the sociopolitical reasons discussed by the traditional exegetes. The affective power of the poem lies in Du Fu's skillful refashioning of standard poetic formulae. He evokes some of the most sacrosanct figures in Chinese mythology and an enduring convention long associated with spiritual uplift and poetic inspiration, only to have them serve as vehicles of despair and frustration. The mood is powerful if unexpected. As in the poem on Daming Palace, Du Fu goes well beyond the requirement of occasional verse composed on a pleasant outing.

In posterity Chu Guangxi and his poem are eclipsed by the giants who were his companions on this excursion. In his own day, however, he was their equal and known as an accomplished poet who excelled in nature poetry.[28] His version of the "Ascent to the Stupa of Compassionate Mercy" is as follows:

> The gold shrine rises in this abode of Arhats;
> Heading straight to the blue clouds' edge.
> The place is quiet, I too am at ease;
> Ascending it in the season of clear autumn.
> The lush greenery is Yichun Gardens;
> The patch of emerald, Lake Kunming.
> Who says that the Heavenly River is high?
> Our rambling is exactly here.
> The illusory universe, a guest of the absolute.
> With joined hands we walk up the azure summit.
> Thunder and tempest along the murky depth;
> Ghosts and spirits within squirm.
> Our spirit changes in an instant;
> None can fathom the sky's end.
> Above our caps, the gates of heaven unfold;
> Under our feet, wild geese fly.
> The chambers of palaces, all in a row;
> The cluster of mountains, so alike.
> Look up, look down, the universe is void.
> Thus let us follow this revelation and return.
> This summit is not a great building;
> To remain for long is thought perilous.[29]
> (1398)

Chu Guangxi too views the excursion as a spiritual pilgrimage. Beginning on a lightsome note of expectancy, the poem moves to a vision of the universe as vast as it is fearsome. Chu develops the topos of ascent by positing two levels of experience; the pleasurable ascent to a safe height

Poetry in a Social Context 59

where the world is attractively telescoped and still conceivable to the human mind, and the ascent to an elevation that defies human comprehension. Infinitude excites more fear than pleasure.

It is generally felt that Chu Guangxi's version is the weakest of the four extant poems. Chu alone does not avail himself of the images of autumn and the Five Mounds to conjure the sense, so pivotal to Buddhist thought, of the vanity and ephemerality of life. Instead he chooses to evoke the Buddhist emphasis upon vastness and vacancy. He is not always successful; felicitous couplets (eg., lines 17-18) are interspersed with lines whose sentiments are somewhat jejune. The most glaring example is the platitudinous last couplet, which states that it is dangerous to remain at the summit for too long.

In contrast to Chu Guangxi's limpid if sometimes bland style, Cen Shen describes the journey to the top in hyperbolic terms:

38. Ascending the Stupa of the Temple of Compassionate Mercy with Gao Shi and Xue Ju

The form of the spire seems to swell up;
Its lone height soars to the palace of the
 gods.
We ascend leaving the world of men;
The precipitous ledge coils around empty
 space.
Thrusting up, it weighs down upon this
 sacred land;
High and jagged like the work of immortals.
Its four corners block the white sun;
Its seven stories brush the sky's canopy.
Squinting down, we point to the birds on high;
Harkening below, we hear the shrill wind.
Mountain ranges like billowy waves,
Rush as if heading to the court of the east.
Green locusts line the wide road;
A honeycomb of palaces and mansions.
The shades of autumn come from the west.
Glaucous grey fills the land within the pass.
The Five Mounds upon the northern plateau,
An eternity of nebulous green.
The pure laws can now be apprehended.

Good causes I've revered early.
I pledge to hang up my official cap;
Relying on the way to awareness, so inexhaustible.³⁰ (2037)

Like his version of the "Morning Audience at Daming Palace," this poem is marked by a full and finished treatment of the designated theme. Cen's compositions on both occasions offer interesting comparisons with those of Du Fu. While Du takes the occasions to make intensely personal utterances, Cen produces exemplary social verse.

The descriptive sequence of this poem follows the visitor's progress up the monument. The first couplet offers a ground-level view of the structure jutting upward, while couplets 2 and 3 depict the ascent. The next five pairs of lines are an account of the view at the summit from all possible angles; the reader is invited to look skyward (couplet 4), downward to the ground (couplet 5), and then into the distance in the four directions, from the mountain ranges in the east (couplet 6), then possibly to the great Tianmen Road south of the temple (couplet 7), westward to the pass (couplet 8) and finally to the Five Mounds in the north (couplet 9). The vantage point affords an expanded view not only of space but also of time, for whereas the south is still green with the summer leaves of the locust trees, autumn can already be seen making its inevitable appearance from the west. Autumn is the season of decline; and so the view shifts from everlasting mountain ranges and splendid buildings to that symbol of mortality, the Five Mounds. A pleasant excursion becomes the occasion of a serious spiritual journey. The concluding avowal to renounce the world, while not original, is an appropriate finale to the poem.

Consistently extolled for his technical skill and exquisitely wrought lines in traditional poetics, Cen's composition on this Buddhist shrine is usually considered to be, after Du Fu's, the most accomplished of the four pieces. Native scholars remark on the deft transition from the physical to the spiritual planes between couplets 8 and 9, as well as the numerous instances of verbal felicity. The vitality and élan with which Cen launches forth the poem make the first couplet a model of the art of beginning a poem, while the oxymoronic statement of the fifth couplet conveys with elegance the sense of great height. Cen's description of the sky in the fourth couplet is more startling and, perhaps, more contrived than Du Fu's "The seven stars are at the

Dipper, / The sound of the Heavenly River flows westwards," which, despite a catachresis in the second line, has the plain vigor of prose. On the other hand, Cen's evocation of autumn, "The shades of autumn come from the west, / Glaucous grey fills the land within the pass," is, for Shi Buhua, an unparalleled example of vigorous lines that still retain an unforced, natural rhythm.[31] This couplet is acknowledged as being more felicitous than either Du Fu's "Shao Hao moves the clear autumn" or Gao Shi's "The autumn wind arrived last evening." In the final analysis, Cen's version lacks both Du Fu's originality and Gao Shi's classicism. If his ideas are unexceptional, a complete mastery of the art of composition makes his poem a model of the poetry of social discourse.

The Poetry of Parting

Numerically, the most significant body of occasional poetry in Chinese is perhaps the verse farewells to particular persons. Parting in early China was observed with a solemn ceremony which consisted of several rituals, including sacrifices to Zushen or Xingshen, the guardian god of the road, and a farewell banquet called jian. Like many customs, the religious overtones were blurred with the passage of time, while the social occasion became ever more elaborate. In the Tang, the farewell banquets in which the literati participated usually included a round of verse-making.

So numerous were the occasions which demanded verse farewells, this sort of composition was well-nigh reduced to a formula. Yang Zai offers a prescription for regulated verse: the opening couplet should state the theme of the composition; the second couplet attends either to the human situation, the parting, or offers a general statement; the third couplet describes the natural scene, the sentiment, or the situation. Yang notes that the topics of the middle couplets are often reversed; the concluding pair of lines should anticipate reunion or offer words of admonition or consolation.[32] Needless to say, the most memorable farewell poems are precisely those which manage to overturn or to extend the formula. Wang Wei's well-known quatrain "Farewell" begins by describing the forlorn feeling after a friend has left, but concludes with the conventional anticipation of return.[33] On the whole, however, farewell verse conforms at least in part to the scheme adumbrated by Yang Zai. The typical poem of parting contains references to the scene at parting as well as to the sentiments of that moment, to the situation which led to the departure, and to the destination of the traveler. More often than not, the conclusion expresses regret, anticipates reunion, and may offer counsel or consolation. In the most skillful compositions, the external scene (jing) of the farewell or the destination is often matched to the internal emotion (qing) of parting or of traveling, so that the one implies the other. Consequently, description of scene is often dictated by figurative rather than by representational considerations. In a seminal article, Hans Frankel has isolated and discussed the recurrent imagery of the poetry of parting.^{34} There seems to be a sameness about the scene in this body of verse that belies the particularity of place and occasion: dew, spring, autumn, morning, evening, wind, cloud, and dust are among the most common lexical figures of parting. Frankel suggests that these images share a common sense of instability and flux which correlates to the traveler's condition. In addition there are a number of natural images that carry symbolic freight, the most common being the wild goose, associated with letter-bearing, and the willow which lined the roads of the ancient cities and whose name, liu, is a homonym of the word for "detain"; it is, therefore, tendered to the traveler as a gesture of regret. Thus subject is often transmuted to simulacrum.

Cen Shen's farewell poetry can be further subdivided into compositions that adhere to the general format for this poetic category and those pieces which honor the traveler with a discussion of some theme only tenuously related to farewell. We will begin with three poems that conform to Yang Zai's pattern and are, therefore, classical examples of the poetry of parting.

39. Escorting Yang Yuan to Nanhai as Chief of Employees
Pentasyllabic regulated style

You did not choose to be chief of employees
　of this southern province.
Venerable parents live within your house.
Towers and loft buildings are folds of mirage;
Hamlets and villages intermix with mermaids.
The sea is darkened by the rain from the three
　mountains;
Flowers brighten with spring from the Five Ridges.

> This region is filled with precious jade,
> Pray, do not tire of pure poverty.³⁵ (2073)

Nanhai, in modern Guangdong, was a semicivilized region during Cen's day. Appointments to this region were generally signs of extreme disfavor; furthermore, Cen's friend was given one of the lowest offices in the government. Cen firmly refrains from the standard expressions of condolence and regret that the occasion calls for. The first couplet states that his friend must accept the post because he owes it to his aging parents. After putting forth this pious and very Confucian (Ruist) consideration, the second couplet proceeds to describe the exotic and semibarbaric south. With allusions to historical and fictional sources, Cen presents a strange land of mirages and mermaids far removed from the world of Ruist obligations evoked in the first couplet; the Shiji speaks of mirages shaped like buildings in the southern wilderness and fictional sources tell of the jiaoren, strange half-men and half-fish who live in the watery depth of Nanhai, who are excellent weavers and whose tears turn to pearls. The third couplet continues the topic of the last pair of lines, but it also modulates to a new mood: "the sea darkened by the rain" amplifies the watery images of the mirage and mermaid; "three mountains" refers to real peaks near Nanhai as well as the mountains of fairyland. "Spring flowers" in the next line takes us back to the familiar and real world, for it is a recurrent image of Chinese poetry. Yet the return to the familiar occurs in a line which also evokes the Five Ridges, the natural mountain barrier separating the familiar and beloved central region from the semibarbaric south. The unknown and known, the real and fictitious thus alternate. The poem concludes with words of admonition that follow logically from the previous lines. Having evoked the south's rich resources of precious gems through the mermaid image, Cen enjoins his friend to resist the temptation toward corruption. "Pure poverty" brings the poem back to the Ruist world where it had begun. The poem thus comes full circle with the familiar ethos expressed in the marginal couplets enveloping the strange land conjured up in the middle lines. It is, in every sense, a composition of finished artistry.

40. Escorting Yangzi
Pentasyllabic regulated style

A picul of wine by the citadel of Wei;
At the tavern suffer a wine snooze.
Pear blossoms, a thousand trees of snow;
Willow catkins, a myriad wisps of smoke.
Regreting our parting, let's refill the wine
  jar;
Approaching the intersection, I give you a whip.
I watch as you leave on the Ying;
A new moon reaching your home, waxes round.[36]
(2081)

The charming scene depicted here is both figurative and literal. This poem verifies Frankel's contention that imagery expressive of transition and instability dominates the poetry of parting. Cen evokes just such a state of flux with the season changing from winter to early spring and with the image of the evanescent smoke. The changes in the human sphere appear in the third couplet's reference to "parting" and "intersection." With the exception of the round moon, all the images are lineal (willow catkins, wisps of smoke, the whip and the river). The perfect sphere (tuanyuan) connotes reunion in China; the full moon thus furnishes an appropriate if commonplace conclusion. The poem below again has all the conventional elements of the poetry of parting:

41. At Prefect Zhao's Southern Pavilion, I Escort Censor Zheng Returning to the Chancellery
Pentasyllabic regulated style

At the red pavilion, the fragrance of wine vats;
A fair faced youth in embroidered attire.
The stone steps are cold, insects chirp at the
  seats;
The blinds part, rain comes to the couch.
A bell compels, our parting elation quickens;
The strings urge, a tipsy song lengthens.
Trees of the pass should be bare early,
Following you with frosty brows. (2076)

The next three poems are addressed to men who were sent away from the capital. Leaving the hub of the empire in Chang'an was always viewed as a misfortune, and parting under such conditions warranted words of commiseration.

42. Escorting Meng Ruqing Returning to Jiyang Following His Failure in the Examinations
Pentasyllabic regulated style

You've submitted prose-poems until your hair
 is almost white;
You're going home in clothes already threadbare.
In shame you pass the trees of Baling;
Returning, you'll till the fields of Wenyang.
To the guest lodge, few letters from home;
Beside your bed, no wine money.
In vain has this wise court kept a vacant place.
Upon the Ji River, a rustic worthy.[37] (2070)

Meng Ruqing was returning to the region covered by modern Shandong province (where Wenyang and the Ji River were located), which was Confucius's birthplace and home state. Cen presents him as the archetypal Confucian worthy, impoverished and unrecognized, but doggedly dedicated to the ideal of public service. Submission of prose-poems or _fu_ to the throne was a signal of one's willingness to serve in office. The bridge over the Ba River, east of Chang'an, is associated with parting and is frequently evoked in farewell verse. Cen was censured by Huang Zhe[38] of the Song dynasty for the bald reference to money in line 4; Huang cites the examples of many ancient literati who had taken exaggerated measures to refrain from mentioning this vulgar consideration.

The next poem is addressed to the great Wang Changling when he was demoted to Jiangning (near modern Nanjing). Wang's biographies[39] speak of his unrestrained conduct and Yin Fan refers to his scurrilous tongue as well as his wild ways. These were, perhaps, the reason why he suffered a total of three exiles to the south, now chiefly remembered as the occasions for some fine farewell poems by his friends. Among the most celebrated is a quatrain by Li Bo written in 748[40] when he was demoted to Longbiao (in southwest Hunan); the following poem by Cen Shen was written when Wang was appointed Magistrate of Jiangning in 742. Cen was clearly fond of Wang Changling, for he sent several messages to the exiled man through other travelers to the south. This farewell to Wang consequently contains a more strongly felt sense of loss than the correct and temperate utterances of the last four pieces:

43. Escorting Wang Changling Leaving for Jiangning

Pentasyllabic ancient style. Date: 742

With wine before us, mute I cannot speak;
My spirit is low, in grief I escort you.
In these enlightened times, your services are not used.
Your hair is white, your learning fruitless.

To the watery region goes one official;
A myriad miles of glaucous waves.
Lordlings fill the gate towers of the capital;
Alone you cross the waters of the Huai.

Your former home in Spring Rich Islet;
You remember reclining at the riverside lodge.
Learning of your departure,
Again and again I gaze towards Xuzhou in the south.

At the end of the alley, alone I close my door.
A cold lamp silences the deep room.
The north wind blows upon flurrying snow.
Willingly we had shared robe and coverlet.

When you reach Jingkou,
It will be the season of peach blossoms.
Within your boat many lone inspirations;
Upon the lake plenty of new poems.

The submerged dragon coils deep;
The yellow crane flies tardily.
I cherish your empyrean quality.
Work hard and keep a good appetite.[41] (2032)

The poem can be conveniently divided into six tetrastichs, each marked by a change of rhyme and a shift of topic. The topics covered are (1) the parting banquet; (2) Wang's journey; (3) Wang's destination in the south; (4) Cen's loneliness following his friend's departure; (5) the season turning to spring when Wang arrives at his destination; and (6) concluding words of encouragement.

The apparent artlessness of the final words of consolation, echoing the conclusion of an old folk song,[42] conceals the considerable art of this poem. Cen offers solace with the following strategy: he draws a contrast between the wintry north (lines 13-16) and the vernal south (lines 17-20), the land which had inspired so many poems. Wang's exile takes him to a land of peach blossoms and spring islets that would quicken his imagination, while Cen is left only with a sense of loss in the dreary north. The poem ends with the customary words of consolation expressed through two conventional tropes: "submerged dragon" is a symbol of the worthy out of office while "yellow crane" represents the worthy living in retirement. Cen manages to invigorate these well-worn tropes. Since Wang is heading toward the region of lakes and rivers, and since the previous lines had evoked "watery region" and "glaucous waves," the dead metaphor of the submerged dragon is reanimated. Indeed, "reclining upon the riverside lodge" (line 10) prefigures the dragon since a variant of "submerged dragon" is "reclining dragon" (wolong). In the final couplet the poet turns to a familiar avian image; the yellow crane of "empyrean quality" (qingyun pin) carries the polar association of elevation to high worldly estate and to eremitic purity. Thus Cen's final consolation is two-edged.

44. Escorting Master Fei Returning to Wuchang
Heptasyllabic ancient style

The homing guest of Hanyang grieves for the
 autumn grass.
Leaves fly by the hostelry, in sorrow they are
 not swept away.
Autumn doubles memories of the Wuchang fish.
Dreams stay only on the Baling road.

You served your commander and traversed Jilian.
Ten years away from home, always at the frontier.
Your sword's point, alas, blunted for a fruitless
 cause;
Your horse's hooves, now worn bare to no avail.

I know how your house was open, how often you
 welcomed guests;
A cast of dice at shupu, a thousand pieces of
 gold.
All your life, you've freely given of your wealth.
The gardens of your home on the river, four bare

walls.

I behold you, Master Fei, your face is extra-
ordinary;
Bushy brows, large mouth, a ruddy moustache.
I watch you go astray like this;
Truly unpredictable are men's fortunes.

In the eighth month of autumn you return to Chu
in the south;
A jar of wine at the east gate poured to the road
god.
Your route points to the northern clouds of Mt.
Phoenix;
Your robes moistened by the shore rain of Parrot
Island.

Do not sigh in despair for white hair new grown.
Keep to the right way, do not be ashamed of poverty.
How can a stalwart lad dote on wife and son?
Do not head for the river hamlet and reject all
men.[43] (2054)

Master Fei's destination is Hanyang across the Yangzi from Wuchang (modern E'cheng, Hubei). Despite the particularity of person and place, the description of Master Fei singles out traits that conform to an established norm; he is seen as the typical knight-errant (yuxia), ready to put his sword and his purse at the disposal of anyone who needs them. As his facial features (lines 13-14) all have literary or historical antecedents, Master Fei is a composite portrait of the stalwart man. Once again, subject is made into simulacrum.

The poem is marked by the regularity and meticulousness of composition that we have come to expect of Cen Shen. Like the farewell to Wang Changling, this piece can also be divided into six tetrastichs, each marked by a change of rhyme and a new topic; these are (1) the hostelry where the farewell takes place; (2) Master Fei's past military career; (3) his past magnanimity and present destitution; (4) his impressive appearance which belies his ill fate; (5) his return home; and (6) admonition and consolation. In accord with the heroic dimensions of the man to whom the poem is addressed, the diction has a manly plainness and forthrightness. Cen eschews the exquisite sentiments delivered in refined poetic language, and he repudiates, in the final couplet, the two occasions that have furnished the inspiration for so many poems - the lament of the forsaken woman and the recluse's rejection of the world. In this composition he honors the manly and stalwart values that tend to be undermined in Chinese poetry by the interest in eremitic ideals and the feminine figure.

The two previous poems appear to be addressed to men for whom the poet felt genuine affection and concern. Social custom in medieval China, however, required the composition of verse even when such feelings were not engaged. Verse farewells are considered <u>de rigueur</u> for the farewell parties, no doubt as numerous as they were tedious, when colleagues and chance acquaintances were transferred or delegated to other places. It would have been considered uncivil for an established literatus like Cen Shen to fail to consecrate such gatherings in verse. Sincerity and veracity of feeling could seldom be summoned to the aid of inspiration on such routine social occasions. Yet an accomplished poet also had too much pride in himself and in his art to fall back always on the hackneyed expressions in a perfunctory exercise. Cen, who had always strained for novel and startling effects, evolved his own distinctive poetic solution to these obligatory compositions.[44] Instead of rendering the farewell in the standard, comprehensive manner described by Yang Zai, he often chose to single out one particular component of this multi-faceted theme for exhaustive treatment. His favorite solution and the one which he used to most original effect is the description of the scene where the parting took place. It is generally acknowledged in traditional poetics that Cen's genius lies in rendering the external scene rather than the internal sentiment.[45] His expressions of farewell thus appear in some remarkable depictions of landscape, as in the two examples below:

45. The Song of Blue Gate: Escorting Administration Officer Zhang of the Chancellery
Heptasyllabic ancient style

The gilt lock of Blue Gate opens at dawn;
The sun rises over the city, an envoy's
 carriage returns.
Willow catkins by the Blue Gate are ripe
 for plucking;

Beside the road, how many partings each day!
Leaving Blue Gate in the east is a road
 without end;
Public trees by post houses, east of Baling.
Flowers flutter upon the traveler's robe,
 they look like embroidery;
Clouds trail after the ongoing horse, you'd
 think it was a piebald.
A Tartar maid in the tavern before high noon;
Silken roped jade vat with milky wine.
At Batou, fallen flowers sink under the horse's
 hooves;
In last night's shower, the flowers become mud.
A yellow oriole with sodden wings, flies
 circling low;
Letters from the east of the pass, too tipsy to
 write.
In a second I'll look and not see you.
A cracking whip, flying saddle, fleet as an arrow.
Oh Envoy, when will you come home?
Don't be the north-flitting shrike or west-
 flitting swallow. (2052)

Blue Gate, also known as the Bacheng Gate, was the eastern gate of the capital of Chang'an; it led to the famous Ba Bridge mentioned in so many parting poems.

The many farewells Cen said to departing colleagues while he was stationed in Anxi furnished him with the opportunity to write about the desertscape which enthralled him and inspired him to new heights of verbal daring. The following poem is one example:

46. The Song of the Clouds of Fire Mountains: In Farewell
Heptasyllabic ancient style

Fire Mountains jut at Chiting's entrance.
At the Fire Mountains in the fifth month, fire
 clouds thicken.
Fire clouds fill the mountains, condensed they
 do not disperse.
Flying birds within a thousand miles dare not come.
At dawn they are suddenly banished, cut off by the
 Tartar wind;
At dusk they all follow the frontier rain and return.

> With sinuous swirls, aslant they engorge the trees
> of Iron Pass.
> Their hazy mist half conceals the garrison of Jiaohe.
> Far reaching the road east of the Fire Mountains;
> Over the mountains, a lone cloud follows your
> horse.[46] (2052)

Cen Shen's attempt to find his individual voice within the communal poetic discourse is not fully convincing. So total is his immersion in the scene, the human feelings seem to be an afterthought tacked on with little conviction to the conclusion; the lone cloud which follows the traveler's horse is an uneasy effort to integrate the natural scene and the human situation. Cen, no doubt, wished as much as Du Fu in the Daming Palace and Buddhist stupa poems to align public obligation to private interests, to make his timbre heard within the chorus. If his particular solution fails sometimes to meet the highest standard of poetry as an organic unity, it nevertheless affords him a means of avoiding the jejune, stereotyped verses that make up the majority of these public performances. Some of Cen's most original frontier poems were composed in farewell. Since these compositions deserve critical attention because of the poet's descriptive genius rather than his public rhetoric, they belong to the next chapter.

Chapter Four
Frontier Poetry

Frontier-style (biansaiti) poetry traditionally designates the compositions about the northern and northwestern frontiers that were the battlegrounds between the Chinese and the nomadic tribes throughout the centuries. Covering a range of attitudes from the eulogistic to the elegiac, and a variety of themes from description of arms and the desertscape to the lament of the soldier and of his loved ones, frontier verse is one of the major thematic categories of Tang poetry. Its antecedents are as old as Chinese poetry itself; the panegyrics to victorious generals, the songs of the aging soldier, and the description of the conscripted man's deserted homesteads have been with Chinese poetry since the Shijing. Han folk songs such as "Fighting South of the Citadel," "Entering the Frontier," and "The Willow Branch," as well as the northern folk songs dating from the Period of Division (420-581), may also be considered precursors of frontier poetry. It was not until the High Tang, however, that this thematic body came to maturity. Well over a thousand compositions about the frontier appear in the Complete Tang Poetry. The theme enjoyed such currency that it was used as an examination topic for the jinshi degree.[1]

The popularity of frontier poetry was related to factors beyond the purely literary. In the early years of the Tang, there was a shared interest between ruler and ruled in maintaining peace on the frontiers. When Li Yuan (posthumous temple name, Gaozu) established the Tang dynasty in 618, it was just two hundred years since the Xiongnu overran northern China. The memory of two centuries of schism could not have been easily forgotten. Gaozu himself had been forced to consider abandoning Chang'an in the wake of a Turkish attack.[2] The hundred years between Gaozu's rule and Xuanzong's accession to the throne in 713 were marked by a series of military campaigns against the Turks, the Tuyouhun, the Koreans, and the Tibetans. Xuanzong's own rule began with victories over the Tibetans and, later on, over the Khitans. By his second reign era, the tianbao, the empire was enjoying such unprecedented prosperity and stability that the emperor proclaimed a program to "totally expel the four barbarians."[3] His militant posture had much popular support at first. Poems from this period consistently note that the traditional diplomatic measures had brought little permanent peace; Gao Shi writes: "We must make the tribes fear us, / And not dare squint at our marriage alliances."[4] The military expansion that responded to these sentiments resulted in almost half a million men and some 80,000 horses being stationed in the nine military commanderies of the empire.[5] The avowed reason for these exercises was to maintain peace. The unspoken but no less pressing motive was the need to keep the northwestern trade routes open by controlling the tribes and so allow for the uninterrupted supply of luxury items from the Middle East to enter China, for the Chinese during the Tang had acquired a taste for the Central Asian material culture. As the many exotica flooded the marketplaces of the great Tang cities from abroad,[6] the frontier ceased to be just the barren and unappealing battleground depicted in earlier poetry. Tang poetry repeats the traditional view, but often it is conjoined with lively descriptions of the vigorous frontier life, the heady Central Asian wine, and its spirited music. The frontier was thus humanized and became an enriched ingredient for the alembic of the poetic imagination.

The lives of the Tang literati were directly affected by the military expansion. Unemployed and frustrated men of letters discovered that they could often find work in some secretarial capacity on the large staffs of the military governors, many of whom were non-Chinese and almost illiterate. Such posts were hardly the first choice of the proud if impoverished literatus. It meant leaving one's home and for some, the amenities of the capitals, for a job which often carried no official ranking. Yet it was a means of eking out a living and held the possibility, however remote, of riding the crest of the general's success to better things. Thus to the enrichment of Chinese poetry, some of the most distinguished names of the age gained a personal knowledge of frontier life. For most of these men it was an experience that they would willingly have forgone. The lowly literatus-secretary or clerk like Cen Shen must have looked upon the honors being showered upon the great frontier generals such Gao Xianzhi, Feng Changqing, Geshu Han, and, above all, An Lushan with a mixture of incredulity and mortification. Their upbringing had not prepared them for this new hawkish emphasis. The time-honored bias toward <u>wen</u>, cultural accomplishment, over <u>wu</u>, martial attainment, seemed largely overturned in this age of promilitary sympathies. Cen Shen was one of many Tang literati who voiced the unorthodox opinion that a man of ambition would have done better to attend to the martial rather than the literary arts:

> In middle age I learn to compose military
>   dispatches;
> I cannot write literary essays.
> A career must accord with the times;
> There is a season for emergence and another
>   for withdrawal.[7]

Gao Shi tells of triumphant generals deriding the scholars: "One canonical text is hardly exhaustive."[8] It seemed at that time that fame and fortune were more readily won on horseback than in the council chamber.

Thus frontier poetry thrived during this brief period when the traditional misgivings about military aggression seemed suspended. The pro-war sentiments were not to last, nor was the voice of pacifism totally silenced even during the heyday of military sympathy. In 750 Du Fu wrote the "Ballad of the Army Carts" and the "Leaving the Frontier" suite[9] in protest against the drafting of reservists and volunteers to fight the Tibetans. High Tang frontier poetry is more vigorous than the simplistic encomia of the early Tang because it succeeds in presenting the war experience in all its contradictory fullness. By the last years of the <u>tianbao</u> era the Tang house had, in the popular opinion, exceeded the line between justifiable war and unrighteous expansionism. And so the traditional repudiation of warring acts returned to poetry and abated the popularity of frontier verse. The number of frontier compositions dating to the Middle and Late Tang was considerably smaller than during the two earlier periods. The reader of Chinese poetry will, of course, find many gems of war poetry written in the centuries after the Tang. Never, however, was the frontier sung of more exquisitely and more spiritedly in so many compositions of one period as during the reign of Xuanzong.

The Frontier Poets

Although examples of frontier poetry can be found in the works of many of the two thousand individuals represented in the Complete Tang Poetry, Chinese literary historians generally assign six names to the so-called "frontier school" (biansai pai); they are Cui Hao (d. 754), Li Qi (690-751?), Wang Zhihuan (b. 695), Wang Changling, Gao Shi, and Cen Shen.[10] "Frontier school" may be misleading, for it is a term coined for the convenience of critical discussion sometime after the Song. Although we have poetic exchanges between Wang Changling and Cen Shen, as well as a graphic account in a contemporary source of Wang Zhihuan, Wang Changling, and Gao Shi carousing and verse-making together in a tavern,[11] there is little indication that the six men considered themselves a distinct group bound by either a shared poetic credo or close ties of friendship. Certainly none of the six made an attempt to confine himself to frontier poetry. Wang Changling was as famous for his palace-style "boudoir lament" as for frontier poems. Li Qi was a serious student of Taoism and wrote some exquisite nature poetry. Numerically, frontier poems account for less than one-fourth of Cen's total extant works.

Few poems have come down to us from Cui Hao, Wang Zhihuan, or Li Qi, who are now remembered only by one or two anthology pieces. It is likely that they had written much more. While he makes no reference to Cen Shen's or Gao Shi's contributions to martial poetry, Yin Fan calls Cui Hao's works "the last word about journeying to the war regions."[12] This suggests that Cui's output of frontier poems might at least have equaled that of Cen and Gao in his day. Of the men who left behind a substantial number of poems, Wang Changling's fame rests upon both frontier-style and palace-style verse, especially those in the heptasyllabic quatrain form. Wang's life is but sketchily outlined in the Tang histories; and there is now no firm evidence to show that he was ever in the far north or west.[13] Possibly his descriptions of the frontier are pure products of the imagination. Cen Shen's and Gao Shi's knowledge of the frontier, on the other hand, is well documented. Both men served for extended periods on the staffs of the powerful military commanders of the day. Gao, under Geshu Han, appears to have gone as far west as Hexi.[14] Cen Shen's peregrinations were even more extensive. Among the six "frontier poets," his knowledge of the western region was unique. A recent survey of place names that appear in the works of the six poets shows that Cen mentions places hardly ever recorded in poetry.[15] Chinese scholars themselves have long acknowledged Cen's original contribution in this area. More than any other subject, the frontier accommodated Cen's search for the new and the startling in poetry.

The unfamiliar world which Cen found in the far northwest and which he endeavored to capture in poetry challenged him with poetic problems. Classical Chinese poetry is generally not receptive to new materials, for its most enduring conventions tend always to reinforce existing matters. Central to classical poetry is the notion of a correspondence between microcosm and macrocosm, the universe and man. Internal human conditions are correlated with external nature in ways that yield endless and provoking interactions. We have already seen in the poetry of parting how the natural object is often both a part of the phenomenal world and an embodiment of an inner human attribute. While this network of associations, evolved through a long poetic tradition, confers upon Chinese poetry both polysemous complexity and fearful symmetry, it is also reductive since it discourages the introduction of elements not invested with accepted association or symbolic import. Nor indeed can the new, uncharged images compete in significance with tropes whose mere names conjure up a wealth of suggestions accrued through the ages. No such meaning lies encapsulated in the unknown Central Asian landscape, whose significance must be explored and developed within each composition. Traditional scholars have sometimes observed that Cen's poetry lacks affective power.[16] This is a price he paid for the daring repudiation of traditional limits.

In choosing novel scenes beyond the Chinese empire for poetic consideration, Cen Shen is also forced to refashion some of the basic strategies of the Chinese lyric. In a real sense, shi poetry is an affirmation of continuity. Poet and reader join in a communion of imaginative exercise as the poet's variation of a familiar theme stirs his reader's memory of other contexts of that theme, and thus excites him with the recognition that an enduring tradition has acquired a new statement. Paying due heed to the continuity of experience between poet and reader, Chinese poetics evolved a principle that would entertain the active participation of the reader in the making of the poetic moment. A recurrent tenet is that the meaning of a poem transcends the text. Sikong Tu (837-908) writes of capturing the spirit without writing a word,[17] while Yan Yu (ca. 1200) looks for the inexhaustible meaning within the finite word.[18] The poetry which reflects this canon is open-ended, indeterminate, and resonant, extending beyond its physical bounds to the actualization of different readers. Shared knowledge and experience are the requisites for the reader's participation in the creation of the poetic moment. Because it deals with a land hitherto unrecorded in poetry and unknown to most of his contemporaries, Cen's frontier poetry is less shared than special, less common than extraordinary. Unable to presume upon the reader's personal response, he also cannot satisfy completely the demand for resonance over sound, indeterminacy over certitude. For this reason, perhaps, traditional poetics have observed that Cen's compositions sometimes lack "far-reaching resonance."[19]

Cen Shen's attempt to integrate his new experience into tradition is apparent in the discussions of the poems which follow. He could not, of course, completely repudiate his poetic lineage. The language available to him was not so much a matter of free choice as a style dictated to him by his own training and the general temper of the day. He knew well that simply to submit his creative impulse to the demands of tradition would mean producing a mere stereotype. On the other hand, should he willfully ignore these demands, his poem would fail as an instrument of communication, and if the poem is meaningless to others, it is also essentially meaningless to himself as social and cultural being.

Poems on Frontier Life

We will begin with a composition which Cen's biographers have assigned to the time of his departure for Anxi with Gao Xianzhi. Hence, it may be one of the earliest pieces Cen wrote of his frontier experiences:

47. On First Passing Long Mountain: Presented to Administrative Officer Yuwen on the Road
Pentasyllabic ancient style.
Date: ca. 750

One post stop and then another;
The post horse like a meteor.
Starting from Xianyang at dawn,
Reaching the foot of Long Mountain at dusk.
The waters of the Long must not be heard;

Its moaning makes one gloomy.
Sand and dust dash against my horse's sweat;
Fog and dew harden my leopard coat.
Who comes from the west?
He says he is newly knighted.
"Last month I started from Anxi,
And did not dawdle on the way.
The commander has not yet arrived.
When I left he was still in Xizhou.
In ten days I crossed the sandy desert;
All morning long the wind did not die down.
My horse galloped over loose gravel,
His four hooves streaming with blood.
A myriad miles on my sovereign's service;
I seek nothing for myself."
I too know the frontier's hardship;
How can I plan for wife and son?
At the mouth of the mountain, a moon emerging,
Shines first upon the citadel's loft building.
The torrent's flow and the wind in the pines,
In the silent night rustle and swish.
Leaving home, I rely upon the dream of return;
In mountains and frontiers, much parting care.
I clasp your hand,
No longer gloomy about the long road ahead. [20]
(2024)

This long poem recounts a meeting at the Long Mountain with an officer of a frontier general. The officer is a stranger but by the end of the poem we find the two men sharing a bond of dedication to duty. The thirty lines can be equally divided into three sections: lines 1 to 10 describe the poet's journey from Xianyang, just northwest of Chang'an to Mt. Long. The next section (lines 11-20) consists of the officer's own account of his journey from Anxi near modern Kucha to the Long Mountain; riding with such fury, he has left his commander behind at Xizhou (Qoco). The last five couplets return to the lodge at Long where the moon and the night wind intensify the two travelers' nostalgia and seal them in a nexus of sympathy and dedication.

The dramatic framework serves at least two purposes: in one sense the poem is an artful account of the poet's journey from Chang'an to Anxi, for the stranger is returning from the region toward which the poet is heading. The account of his itinerary thus supersedes the description of

Frontier Poetry 79

the later stages of the poet's journey. The dramatic structure thus serves to break up the monotony of a straightforward and heavy-gaited narrative. The meeting also represents an encounter between experience and innocence. By the end of the poem, the seasoned officer has instilled the novice with new fortitude so that the latter can disavow the gloom which had overtaken him at the beginning of the poem.

Within the three sections of the poem, Cen evokes the Han folk ballads "Waters of Longtou" and "Chant of Longtou,"[21] which describe the gloom of the mountain stream and the matching despondency of the traveler to the north. He also evokes (in lines 22-26) images that conventionally suggest desolation: the wind among the pines, the dream of home in a moon-drenched night. Sandwiched between these familiar images and sentiments, however, is an account of the frontier that is as harsh as it is unfamiliar. The blood streaming from the horse galloping over miles of rocks is much more brutal than the ubiquitous "sand and dust dash against my horse's sweat." "In ten days I crossed the sandy desert; / All day long the wind did not die down," is again more relentless than the conventional depiction of the wind in the pines "rustling and swishing in the silent night." The genteel dejection which customarily imbues poems on the frontier seems too tame a response to the brutality of the harsh land that bordered the Tang empire.

A similar tension between the poetic convention and the real frontier occurs in the following poem about Mt. Silver Desert (Kumush), located northeast of Karashahr:

48. The West Lodge of Mt. Silver Desert
Heptasyllabic ancient style. Date: 750

At the mouth of Mt. Silver Desert, the wind is
　like an arrow;
West of Iron Gate Pass, a moon like floss.
Pair by pair, gloomy tears soak my horse's mane.
Sough-swishing Tartar sand cracks my face.
A man at thirty who has not achieved fame and
　fortune,
Can hardly pore over his studies day by day.
(2056)

Although the poem appears in the Complete Tang Poetry among the heptasyllabic ancient-style compositions, it is actually an obscure variant of regulated verse known as the "short form regulated verse with three rhyme words (sanyun xiaolu)."[22] The form follows the rules of regulated verse in terms of rhyme, tonal pattern, and antithesis, but it omits one couplet.

Cen is probably describing the scene around the Luguang Lodge, located some forty li from Karashahr.[23] The poem begins with two parallel couplets whose antitheses highlight the tension between the expressions of despair sanctioned by poetic convention and the descriptions which originate from the poet's own experience. The flosslike moon that brings forth tears of sorrow belongs to convention, but the wind stirring gritty sand that cracks human skin has a violence seldom known in the polite and moderate world of Chinese letters. The antitheses pitch the gentle "soak" against the savage "crack," and rhyme the piercing "arrow" (tsian) with the soft "floss" (lien). The polarity reveals the inadequacy of traditional poetic imagery and lends conviction to the final assertion that in this merciless land, the Chinese emphasis upon cultural accomplishment is indeed inappropriate.

Some miles south of Mt. Silver Desert and west of Karashahr is a narrow defile which the ancients called Iron Gate Pass. Official Chinese histories describe an awesome mountain that looks as if "an ax had fallen between the two sides of the defile."[24] At the beginning of this century, Sir Aurel Stein reports that at its narrowest point "a wooden gate across the road, with troglodyte quarters for a guard, marks a watch station still in being."[25] Cen inscribed a poem there:

49. Inscribed on the Loft Building of Iron Gate Pass
Pentasyllabic ancient style

Iron Gate at the western end of the sky;
As far as the eye can see, few travelers.
A tiny officer at the gate of the pass,
All day long faces a wall of rock.
The bridge straddles the thousand feet
 height;
The road girts the steep defile.
Trying to climb the west loft building
 to look,
One look is enough to turn my hair white. (2046)

The poem reiterates three qualities: height ("rock wall," "thousand feet height," "climb," "loft building"), infinite space ("as far as the eye can see," "western end of the sky"), and infinitesimal man ("few travelers" and "tiny officer"). Synonymous words, thus reiterated to gathering intensity, convey a sense of the monolithic quality of the pass.

50. Composed in the Desert
Heptasyllabic quatrain

My galloping horse comes to the west, almost
  reaching the sky.
Since leaving home, twice has the moon waxed
  round.
Tonight I don't know where I'll sleep.
A myriad leagues of level sand, cut off from
  human smoke. (2106)

This quatrain can be dissected in two ways. On the one hand the marginal and center lines attract. Lines 1 and 4 describe infinite space, while 2 and 3 attend to the lot of finite man. On the other hand, odd and even lines cohere; line 2 speaks of longing for home while line 4 exceeds this conventional sentiment by stating that the traveler is not only deprived of the solace of home, but of all human contact. Similarly, the odd-numbered lines are drawn to each other in statements of the twin aspects of traveling, riding by day (line 1), and finding lodging by night (line 3).

Some of the most striking pieces about the frontier by Cen Shen have as their subject the Fire Mountains near Turfan. The mountains lie on a major fault line dividing the Turfan Depression, which is itself a fault trough north of the Qurug Tag Mountain. At its lowest point, the trough descends to some 505 feet below sea level while surrounding areas bordering the Tarim River and Lop-nor Lake are between 2,000 and 3,000 feet above sea level. The area has great climatic extremes.

51. On Passing the Fire Mountains
Pentasyllabic ancient style

Today, the first sight of the Fire Mountains;
Jutting forth east of Fuchang.
Russet flames burn the caitiff clouds;

Smoking vapors steam the frontier void.
Who knows why the coals of yin and yang,
Ignite this region alone?
I came in stern winter;
Below the mountains, much smoking wind.
Men and horses drained of sweat.
How can one know the might of creation?[26]
(2046)

52. At Wuwei I Escort Administrative Officer Liu Leaving for Jixi to Join the Army
Heptasyllabic quatrain

At the Fire Mountains in the fifth month,
   travelers are scarce.
I watch your horse speed away, swift as a bird.
The commander-in-chief is bivouacked west of
   Taibo.
A tremor of the horn, the Tartar sky dawns.
(2104)

Jixi, also known as the Jubilou desert, is located west of Anxi. Administrative Officer Liu's route takes him through the mercilessly hot Turfan Depression in the height of summer. Cen begins by observing that few travelers venture to cross the Turfan Depression in June, but that his stouthearted friend plans to forge ahead with the speed and ease of a bird in flight. Because of the great heat, he will begin his journey before dawn. Taibo in line 3 is the name of several mountains, none of which is located on the traveler's route from Wuwei (in Gansu) to Jixi. It may refer to the star Venus, whose special significance for war is mentioned in many Tang poems. Cen's spare, almost stark diction complements the bleak land through which the traveler passes. The last line, depicting dawn breaking out over the desert, is remarkable. Freezing that evanescent instant that melts no sooner than it comes into being, the line seals the momentary now from the relentless march of time.

    Much of Cen Shen's time in Feng Changqing's service was spent at Luntai (modern Bugur), near Anxi. The fact that he could not contribute to Feng's military successes during this period and that he was not included in the summons to return to Chang'an following the outbreak of civil war,

Frontier Poetry 83

accounts perhaps for the sense of frustration and ennui that fills the following poems about life at Luntai:

53. Serving at Luntai
Pentasyllabic regulated style.
Date: 754-56

The scenery at Luntai is strange;
This was the land of the ancient khans.
In the third month, there's no green grass;
Before a thousand homesteads, all white elms.
The language of barbarian missives is different;
The speech of the Tartar populace is dissimilar.
Despondent, I look north of the flowing sands –
A corner of a lake west of the sky.[27] (2091)

54. At Luntai at the Beginning of Autumn
Pentasyllabic regulated style. Date: 756

In a strange land beyond the Yin Mountain;
At a lonely citadel beside the snowy lake.
Autumn comes with only the wild geese;
Summer ends without hearing cicadas.
The rain brushes the rug tapestry and it is wet;
A wind wafts the felt tent and it stinks.
At Luntai, a myriad miles away,
With nothing to do I've passed three years.[28]
(2090)

In these two pieces Cen combines the familiar and the unfamiliar; the former serves to anchor the poems in a shared frame of reference, whereas the latter bends the established framework to accommodate his new experience. Thus, in "At Luntai at the Beginning of Autumn," both lines of the third couplet begin by evoking the gentle movements of nature celebrated in countless Chinese lyrics ("the rain brushes" and "the wind wafts"). The second half of the lines, however, depicts phenomena of nomadic life totally unknown in Chinese poetry. The unique Luntai ambience acquires a degree of familiarity in several ways: (1) by negation. Luntai is described through the absence of objects commonly found in China, such as "no green grass," or "without hearing cicadas." (2) By exclusion. The wild goose and the white elm are just two of the many features within the temperate Chinese landscape, whereas in desolate Luntai they are the sole objects. (3) By thwarting stock responses. The act of gazing into the distance is common in classical poetry; looking "north of the flowing sands" (line 7), however, does not yield the expected panoramic view, but the tunnel vision of "a corner of the lake." The effect is one of the strange within the ordinary. As in nearly all of his compositions, Cen's attempt to describe his unique experiences in the west drives him constantly to strain the fixities of conventional poetry, but just as consistently, he stops short of openly destroying the established patterns.

Some of the most charming of Cen Shen's frontier poems are on tribal music. Cen's interest reflects the taste of his day, for the popularity of the non-Chinese music was so great in the Tang, it furnished the entertainment for parties at many Chang'an mansions. Thus, when the great scholar-calligrapher Yan Zhenqing (709-785)[29] left on a tour of inspection of Helong (Hexi and Longyou, the area covered by modern west Gansu, eastern Xinjiang, and northeast Qinghai), he was escorted by the strains of the Tartar pipe (hujia). Cen made the pipe the theme of a most original farewell poem:

55. Song of the Tartar Pipe: Upon Escorting Yan Zhenqing Appointed to Helong
Heptasyllabic ancient style. Date: 748

Do you hear, Sir, how sad is the sound of the
  Tartar pipe?
Purple bearded and green eyed, the Tartar who
  plays it.
He plays and the song is not finished,
Whelmed with gloom is the soldier lad of Loulan.
In the cool autumn of the eighth month, on the
  Xiao Pass road,
The north wind snaps the Tianshan grass.
South of Mt. Kunlun, a moon slanting;
The Tartar turns to the moon and plays the
  Tartar pipe.
Plaintive the strains of the Tartar pipe that
  escorts you.
At the Qin mountain we gaze towards the clouds
  of Long Mountain.
In the frontier citadel, nights of gloomy dreams;
A Tartar pipe turned to the moon - who rejoices
  to hear it? (2053)

Frontier Poetry

The poem consists of twelve lines, eight of which attend to the music of the pipe while the last tetrastich describes the farewell. The themes of music and farewell are ingeniously interwoven.

Within the first eight lines, Cen covers many facets of the pipe: the music it produces (line 1), its performer (line 2), the response to the music (lines 3-4), and the instrument itself, made from the reed grass broken by the harsh Tianshan wind (lines 5-6). In the transitional couplet (lines 7-8), the pipe takes us from the Kunlun Mountain to the farewell banquet in honor of Yan Zhenqing. The farewell is couched with many echoes of the previous lines. Qin and Long mountains in line 10, Yan's point of departure and destination, respectively, complement the reference to Xiao Pass (southeast of modern Guyuan, Gansu), one of the four passes leading out to the frontier route and therefore one of the stops on Yan's itinerary. The next line, "In the frontier citadel, nights of gloomy dreams," evokes line 4, "Whelmed with gloom is the soldier lad of Loulan (Kroraina)." Just as it had begun the poem, a rhetorical question concludes it. The final line not only echoes the opening line with the repetends "Tartar pipe" and "hear," as well as the interrogative construction but it also renews the reader's memory of the transitional eighth line with the repetition of "turned to the moon" and "Tartar pipe." The two words which conclude the poem, "rejoice" (xi) and "hear" (wen), contain a double entendre. "A Tartar pipe facing the moon - who rejoices to hear it?" is the logical conclusion to a poem which had made the pipe embody the sorrows of parting. "Rejoice to hear," on the other hand, also carries a pun on the anticipated "joyous news" of Yan's success on this tour of duty.

In the next poem, Cen Shen describes another fete where the reed pipe or alto oboe (pili)[30] entertains the guests. Like the Tartar pipe, the reed pipe is made of a reed mouthpiece and a bamboo body. It differs from the Tartar pipe in having nine air holes.

56. Song: The Reed Pipe of General Pei's Residence
Heptasyllabic ancient style

In Liaodong in the ninth month, reed leaves break;

Liaodong's children pluck the reed pipes.
Lovely are these new pipes, so clear and sad.
A song drifts in the wind filling the lake's
  far end.

Trees by the lake sigh and sough, the sky
  rains and frosts;
The pipe's strains are light and lilting, the
  moon gris-grey.
Those north of White Wolf River bear gloomy
  grievance;
Those south of Dark Hare Citadel, their hearts
  all break.

In the Chang'an residence of the Liaodong
  general,
A lovely lady with her reed pipe attends
  distinguished guests.
She plays a melody, whistling and whizzing, it
  surpasses the bamboo flageolet;
She begins a note, deep and distant, it
  suppresses the horizontal flute.

Night deepens in the high hall, the guests have
  not yet left.
Just let the reed pipe accompany your cups.
Its art can startle the willow on the path;
Then it can be mistaken for falling plums in
  the orchard.

The many guests love it, they cannot have
  enough.
Pearl blinds unfurled on high, red candles set.
The general in intoxicated dance would not
  retire,
Again he has the lovely lady play a song. (2057)

Liaodong refers to modern southeast Liaoning province, while White Wolf River is located in Liaocheng, Shandong, and Dark Hare Citadel, in southern Kirin, Manchuria. Lines 11 and 12 allude to two well-known songs for wind instruments, the "Willow Branch" and "Plum Blossoms Falling."

To complement the musical theme, Cen maximizes the musical potentials of the poetic language with liberal use of onomatopoeia. The poem contains four pairs of alliterative or rhyming compounds, seu-sak ("sigh and sough"), leu-liang ("light and lilting"), tsiou-sriou ("whistle and whiz"), and geu-dheu ("deep and distant"), as well as one echoic binome, tsang-tsang ("gris-grey"). The compositional framework reflects Cen's habitual attention to balance and symmetry. The twenty lines are distributed among five tetrastichs, two of which describe the pipe as it is made and played in Liaodong, with the other three depicting its performance in the Chang'an residence of a general who had served in that region. The repetition of key words is noteworthy. "Reed pipe" is repeated five times, once in each tetrastich, and Liaodong is mentioned three times, twice in the opening couplet and once in line 9, which marks the transition from Liaodong to Chang'an. "Lovely lady" appears in the transitional and concluding couplets. Regular intervals punctuate regulated lines (7-8, 11-12, 15-16) and pairs of lines which do not observe tonal pattern or antithesis.

Liaodong and Chang'an share the plaintive music of the reed pipe, but in other respects they are at antipodes. Liaodong is desolate, while Chang'an is convivial. As the place names White Wolf River and Dark Hare Citadel suggest, Liaodong is rude, whereas the general's residence in the western capital is equipped with every luxury. Students of the Marxist persuasion may find implied social criticism in the difference between the life-styles of the pampered commanders and the lonely soldiers forced to put in long years of service on the frontier. Cen Shen commits himself neither to an explicit denunciation nor even to a pointed antithesis in the style of the famous couplet from Gao Shi's "Song of Yan:" "Warring men at the battlefront, betwixt life and death; Lovely lady within the tent, yet another song and dance."[31]

The next poem describes a version of the tribal twirl dance (huxuan) which was so popular in Cen's day. A Tang source claims that the dance originated in Samarkand and became such a great favorite that the Maimargh, Kess, and Kumeah tribes all sent tributes of dancers who excelled in the dance to Chang'an.[32] The "twirl" is described as having been performed by two dancers in flamboyant costumes: purple jackets with brocade sleeves, emerald damask trousers, and russet leather boots. One version involved an acrobatic feat of intricate steps executed on a ball.[33] The dance that Cen Shen saw appears to have been a spear dance in which the girls whirled and twirled round the spears which they planted now to the left, now to the right. Arthur Waley accuses the poet of showing bad taste in declaring his preference for such acrobatic displays to the classical style of the Chinese dance.³⁴ We must remember, however, that this composition is an occasional poem composed in honor of his host and that such works demand hyperbolic praise:

57. Song: Commissioner Tian's Lovely Lady Dances "Like the Lotus" Northern Spear Dance
Heptasyllabic ancient style

The lovely lady dances the lotus twirl.
The eyes of men have not seen its like.
The whole floor of the high hall is spread
  with red rugs.
She dances to a melody unlike any other.
This melody the Tartars transmitted to the
  men of Han;
The many guests watch, they exclaim and sigh.
A languid face, coy brows, trim yet buxom,
Buoyant gossamer, gold thread, flowers lushly
  luxuriant.
A turn of her skirt, a twist of the sleeves,
  like flying snow;
A spear to the left, a spear to the right,
  cyclones arising.
The <u>piba</u> and the horizontal flute join and
  before they are finished,
Huamen Mountain is enfolded in yellow clouds.
Suddenly the strains of "Leaving the Frontier"
  and "Entering the Frontier";
White grass and Tartar sand chill swish-swishing.
She turns when the strains grow urgent as if her
  spirit were stirred.
A glimpse of her front, a glimpse of her back,
  each time so new.
Then I know that the other songs cannot vie with
  this;
"Plucking the Lotus" or "Plum Blossoms Falling"
  merely grate the ear.
The world learns to dance and it is just a dance;
Its movements are hardly like this.³⁵ (2057)

Cen Shen was also captivated by the climatic extremes of Central Asia, so different from the orderly progression of the Chinese seasons. In several poems he combines his descriptions of great snowfall and fearful heat with poetic farewells. These poems mark a departure from standard poetic practice which explores the theme of farewell comprehensively, covering scene, sentiment, and situation. Instead, Cen singles out the scene of the parting for sustained description.

58. The Song of the White Snow: Upon Escorting Administrative Officer Wu Returning to the Capital
Heptasyllabic ancient style

The north wind coils the ground, white grass snaps.
Directly from the Tartar sky in the eighth month comes flying snow;
Suddenly like the spring wind coming one night,
And pear blossoms unfold upon the myriad trees,
Scattering into pearl blinds, moistening gossamer curtains.
Fox garments have no warmth, damask beddings grow thin.
The commander's horned bow cannot be drawn;
The protector-general's iron armor so cold and hard to don.
Railings of ice over the desert criss-cross a hundred feet thick;
Gloomy clouds, dull and dreary, seal a myriad leagues.
Within the army headquarters wine is set for the departing guest;
The Tartar lute, the piba and the tribal reed.
Helter-skelter, dusk snow falls upon the main gate.
The wind tugs the red flag, frozen it does not flap.
At the east gate of Luntai, we escort you off;
You leave when snow fills the Tianshan road.
A curve of the mountain, a turn of the road, you are lost to sight,
Leaving only the print of horse hooves on the snowy mountain.[36] (2050)

The poet uses a direct and simple style that minimizes the difference between the grammar of poetry and that of prose. One set of loosely antithetical couplet (lines 7-8) and one example of asyndeton (line 12) are the sole instances of the poetic idiom.

"The Song of the White Snow" is yet another example of the symmetry and balance of Cen Shen's poetic compositions. In eighteen lines he delineates the stages of the snowstorm from its incipience with the rising of the north wind to the gathering coldness (lines 3-8), then to the change from snow to ice (lines 9-10), and finally to the subsiding snow flurry (line 13) and the stillness following the storm (17-18). The eighteen lines can also be divided into two equal sections of eight lines with a transitional couplet separating the two sections. The first section describes the snowfall while the second attends to the departure of Administrative Officer Wu. Lines 9 and 10, depicting the ice which blocks a myriad miles, make an observation on the distance and the icy impediment to travel and thus lead gracefully to the theme of departure in the second section. Images relating to the military camp (lines 7-8 and 13-14), the parting banquet (lines 5-6 and 11-12), and of course the ubiquitous snow interlock the two sections. The bipartite structure of the poem is also contrastive. Beginning with the wind "rolling up" the ground and ending with the accoutrements of the great officers, the perspective of the first eight lines moves from distance to close-up. The last eight lines reverse this sequence, for they begin with the musical instruments played at the banquet and conclude with the panoramic sweep of the snow-filled mountain. Stylistically, the first part moves toward hyperbole and the second toward meiosis. Lines 1 to 10 gather in intensity as the imagery becomes increasingly exuberant; the white pear blossom in line 4, evoking the late snow that coincides with the advent of spring, is a commonplace trope for snowflakes. The following line draws again from the stock poetic repertoire, but line 6 moves beyond gossamer fabrics to describe the inadequacy of fur garments and thick bedding; this conceit exceeds the standard poetic expressions of the cold. The imagery of the ice as <u>langan</u>, "a balustrade," or "in a criss-cross pattern," is unique. It has been variously interpreted as either describing the icicles hanging from the precipices like railings, or the criss-cross pattern of the ice upon the ground. From the stock image of pear blossoms to the original "railings of ice," the effect is one of increasing excess. By way of contrast, the second half of the poem seems to diminish in intensity. Beginning with the boisterous Tartar music, it ends in soundlessness. "Empty print" in the final line takes the reader back to the quiet but familiar world of the recluse evoked so often in the poetry of Cen's time.

Cen Shen was clearly pleased with his description of the snowscape and with its use as an original format for parting verse, for he left another composition on the snow, dedicated also to a departing friend, that repeats the previous piece in imagery, structure, and rhyme scheme:

**59. Song of the Tianshan Snow:
Upon Escorting Xiao Zhi Who
Returns to the Capital**
Heptasyllabic ancient style

There's snow upon Tianshan, often it is not open.
A thousand peaks and a myriad monts of craggy snow.
The north wind coils at night at the mouth of
  Chiting;
All through the night the snow piles thicker.
It joins the Han moon to shine upon Mt. Silver.
It pushes the Tartar wind across Iron Pass.
By Jiaohe's citadel, the flying birds are cut off;
On Luntai's road, horses' hooves slip.
An overcast air congeals a myriad miles.
The railings upon the dark cliff are a thousand
  feet of ice.
The general sleeps in his fox garment with no
  warmth;
The commander's precious dagger is frozen and
  about to snap.
Just as snow falls upon Tianshan,
I escort you on horseback on your return to the
  capital.
In the snow, what is there to give you,
But a branch from the verdant pine?[37] (2051)

The last line is a variation of the traditional custom of presenting the traveler with a willow branch. In the far north this cherished gesture of farewell is improvised with a pine branch.

Cen Shen is equally excited by the intense heat of Central Asia. The following piece is surely one of the most striking poems in classical literature:

60. Ballad of Hot Lake: Escorting Censor Cui Returning to the Capital
Heptasyllabic ancient style

I've heard the Tartar lads of Yin Mountain say,
At the west end of Hot Lake, the water seems to boil.
Above the lake, the flock of birds dares not fly;
Within it are carp long and plump.
Beside the shore, green grass never withers;
In the void, white clouds afar swirl and die away.
Steaming sand, glowing rocks ignite the caitiff cloud;
Bubbling waves, smoking billows fry the Han moon.
A phosphorescent fire burns this cauldron of the universe.
Why does it only bake this western corner?
Its force captures the Moon Cavern, it invades Taibo star.
Its air joins Russet Slope, it reaches the khan.
I escort you in tipsiness to the rim of Tianshan;
Just now we see the evening sun set beside the lake.
The frost of the Censorate awes, its chill intimidates;
The smoking air of the Hot Lake is made to seem paltry.[38] (2051)

Hot Lake is the Chinese name for Lake Issyk-kul in the Kirghiz Soviet Socialist Republic. It is usually assumed that Cen Shen is describing this, the largest of the earth's lakes. Yin Mountain refers to the mountain range spanning Suiyuan, Chahar, and Jehol in the north central and northeast frontiers of China, while Russet Slope is placed by the geographical dictionaries at Longting, Shaanxi. Neither one of these places is located anywhere near Issyk-kul. We may assume that Cen is exercising some degree of poetic license here. "Russet" is a warm color, while "shady" (yin) and "hot" are calorific words that are consistent with the mood of the poem if not the exact topography of the frontier.

The poem begins with a series of seemingly incompatible

Frontier Poetry

statements. Water, associated with a cooling effect, is the source of heat. Birds dare not fly over the lake, yet fishes thrive within its waters. Cloud vapors are burned out by the heat, while green grass flourishes on the shore. These contradictions are a rhetorical means of suggesting a heat that defies human comprehension. On the other hand, there is also something familiar about the heat, for between lines 8 and 10, Cen describes it in a series of culinary terms.

The concluding tetrastich attends to the farewell and the shift of topic is marked by a change from images of heat to those of chill. As the surveillance branch of the government, the Censorate is often described as inspiring chilling fear. The last couplet is deliberately ambiguous because there are two usages of the word wei: as a transitive verb, "to make," and as a coverb, "for the sake of," "for," and "by." The two usages yield opposite meanings in the last line, so that the reader must choose between (1) "The Hot Lake's smoking air makes it (the awe of the Censorate) paltry" or (2) "The Hot Lake's smoking air is made to seem paltry by the Censorate." Traditional commentators, with their ingrained sense of public service, favor the second reading, which indeed would be a more appropriate and tactful adieu to the departing censor. Yet, as poem 6 shows, Cen is quite capable of making an irreverent innuendo.

These examples of Cen Shen's frontier compositions leave no doubt that they are among some of the most forceful and original expressions in Chinese poetry. Their limitations are no less apparent. In the three parting poems, for example, the descriptions of snow and heat, startling and brilliant though they are, contribute little to the human implications of friendship and parting. The themes of farewell in the snow and by the Hot Lake are skillfully interwoven on the compositional level, but they fail to interact in any deep sense on the plane of human emotions. By electing to go beyond the confines drawn by tradition, Cen Shen loses, to some degree, its sustaining powers. The frontier landscape which so captivated Cen is a blank slate empty of affective associations. Consequently, the fullness of those poems in which scene embodies sentiment and the present situation echoes the literary past, often eludes Cen's parting compositions. If a line such as his "The wind wafts the felt tent and it stinks" has instantaneous impact, it yet lacks the power of Wang Wei's "Pine wind blows, loosening my sash," which, to the reader steeped in the Chinese tradition, evokes some of the pivotal concerns of life. This perhaps is one reason why native critics sometimes take exception to Cen for "sacrificing veracity for the sake of clever lines."[39]

Cen Shen himself seems sensible of the problem he faces. In the following poem he makes a belabored attempt to confer meaning on an unknown desert flora. The plant is probably the flower of the Persian variety of the fig, the fruits of which are larger and superior to the Chinese variety grown in the Yangzi region. This blossom has never entered Chinese poetry, hence Cen perceives a correspondence between the anonymous flower and an anonymous official like himself.

61. The Song of the Youbenluo Flower
Irregular ancient style. Date: 756

South of the White Mountain,
North of Russet Mountain,
There is a flower unknown to man.
Green stem, jasper leaves, such lovely hues.
Six petals,
Nine whorls;
Folding by night, unfolding by morn its
  sweet scent unique.
Why does it not grow in the Central Kingdom,
  why in the west?
I moved it to the courtyard,
It graces my office.
Ashamed to be the peer of the various fauna,
How erect it stands in lone fragrance.
Why is it not admired by man?
In deep mountains and remote valleys, it
  submits to the stern frost.
I'm sad that the road to Yang Pass is long,
That I cannot present it to my sovereign.[40]
(2062)

Cen Shen continues to grapple with the twin demands of the poetic tradition he inherited and the fresh insights gathered from his own unique experiences in the compositions on war and warriors. Some of these poems are indifferent exercises. Many, however, are masterpieces of Chinese war poetry.

Frontier Poetry

Poems on War and Warriors

Between the spring of 754 and the eleventh month of 755, Cen Shen wrote a series of poems dedicated to his superior, Feng Changqing. In the winter of 754 Feng conducted a successful campaign against the Charchans which gave Cen an opportunity to offer several poems in celebration of his exploits. The series of compositions which follow are public utterances and they show the decorum and tact demanded in addresses to one's superior:

62. The Song of Luntai: Presented When Escorting My Lord Feng Leaving with His Troops on a Western Campaign
Heptasyllabic ancient style. Date: 754

At Luntai's citadel, the horn sounds at
  night.
North of Luntai's citadel, the Pleiades
  fall.
A feathered dispatch last night crossed
  Quli.
The khan is already west of the Altai
  mountains.
Behold, west of the lookout, smoke and
  dust blacken.
The Han troops are bivouacked north of
  Luntai.
The great general presses his yaktail flags
  forward on the western march.
At dawn to the sound of pipes the great army
  leaves.
From the four sides they beat the drums, the
  Snow Sea surges;
The three divisions raise a warcry, Yin
  Mountain moves.
The martial air of this caitiff frontier
  reaches the cloud clusters.
White bones on the battlefield wrapped by
  grass roots.
By Sword River the wind rages, cloud patches
  disperse;
At Sand Mouth rocks freeze, horseshoes fall.
The Vice Premier, serving his sovereign,
  willingly toils;

> The general under oath, requiting his master,
> cleanses the frontier dust.
> Who has not seen the bamboo annals of antiquity?
> Greater than the ancients are those we look upon today.[41] (2051)

The poem begins by depicting the initial barbarian advance toward Luntai. The first eight lines give the background to the expedition and carefully identify the time and the place; the Chinese troops are stationed north of Luntai while their enemies come from the west. The khan marches by night and the Chinese move at dawn to meet them in battle. The following eight lines evoke the battle between Chinese and barbarians. Cen uses the classical strategy of Chinese war poetry, aptly termed by C.H. Wang the "ellipsis of battle."[42] Description of combat is invariably omitted in shi poetry. It is a point of indeterminacy that awaits actualization in the reader's mind. Combat is implied in a number of ways, chief among them being the displacement of human strife into natural turmoil and the distortion of chronology whereby the scene of carnage following the undescribed battle is treated. Cen avails himself of both strategies in this poem. The surging Snow Sea and the raging Sword River act as objective correlatives of the heat of battle, while the image of the soldiers' bones in line 12 removes the present context to historical time.

The poet builds up the momentum by a graduated energization and elevation of the language. There is a significant shift of diction between the first half of the poem (lines 1-8), which describes the preparation for combat, and the second half (lines 9-18), which attends to the battle itself. The first eight lines eschew the syntactic devices identified with poetic grammar. With the exception of the repetition of "Luntai" in lines 1 and 2, and the verbal usage of the adjectival "black" (line 5), the language of the first lines is little differentiated from that of prose. The poet selects the most ordinary of verbs, zai ("to be at"), in lines 1 and 6; guo ("to cross"), in line 6, in this beginning section. The tedium of the long night prior to the battle is broken in the ninth line. Thenceforth the poet summons forth some of the principal devices of the poetic syntax. Antithesis, scrupulously avoided in the first half of the poem, appears in four couplets (lines 9-16). These later lines are also distinguished from prose by isolative syntax; thus the relationship between the raging Sword River and the widening cloud patches (line 13) is not defined by a causal particle as it would be in classical prose. The resulting parataxis accentuates the metrical rhythm of the regular heptasyllabic line in which the caesura falls after the fourth character: "Sword River wind rages / cloud patches disperse." The later lines are also energized by numerous kinetic verbs. The odd-numbered couplets (lines 9-10 and 13-14) contain two strong verbs of motion in each line. The frenetic pace slackens at the concluding lines as rhyming couplets yield to a rhyming tetrastich which honors Feng Changqing and magnifies his exploits by means of a historical amplification.

A second farewell to Feng Changqing is composed in a wholly different style.

63. The Ballad of Running Horse River: Presented upon Escorting My Lord Feng Leaving with His Troops on a Western Campaign

Heptasyllabic ancient style. Date: 754

Behold, Sir, Running Horse River by the side
of Snow Lake;
A jungle of level sand, yellow enters the sky.

At Luntai in the ninth month, the wind howls
at night;
A river bank of loose rocks, large as bushel
baskets,
Rushes with the wind, rolling all over the
ground.

The Hun grass is yellow, its horses sleek;
Looking westwards from Altai, smoke and dust
fly.
The great general of the Han house leads his
troops westwards.

The general does not doff his metal armor at
night;
At midnight the army marches, lances poke each
other;
The headlong wind like dagger, faces feel
slashed.

Sweat steams from our horses' snow covered hair;

Thereby making ice on "five petal" and "coin
chain" hides.
Within the tent the ink for dispatches freezes
on the slab.

Hearing this the caitiff horsemen must be terror
stricken;
I surmise they would not dare to engage you in
hand combat.
The Jushi at the west gate await you anxiously to
present tributes.[43] (2052)

The style of this poem differs from standard ancient-style verse in several respects. Instead of the usual even number of lines, the poem contains seventeen lines. With the exception of the initial rhyming couplet, rhyme appears at the end of each line with the change of rhyme occurring at the third rather than the customary even-numbered lines. The dominance of the odd number means that the couplet is no longer the basic unit of composition and that such key poetic devices as tonal, grammatical, and semantic antitheses cannot obtain in this composition. Wang Li suggests that the poem's unusual style is derived from the "Boliang style," named after the "Boliang Terrace," an odd-lined poem with rhyme at the end of each line composed by the Emperor Wu of Han and his retainers. Shen Deqian (1673-1769) compares the poem to the "Mt. Yi Inscription," ordered by Qin Shihuangdi to commemorate the achievement of his reign.[44]

The uncommon style is matched by a content that also strains our sense of the expected. Cen completely reverses the traditional connotations of the frontier. The sand, habitually seen as "bare" and "dim", is characterized here by the word mang, which usually describes rank and luxuriant jungle growth. The grass, constantly depicted as dry and funereal white, becomes an image of autumnal abundance in the line, "The Hun grass is yellow, its horses sleek." The barren desert is thus seen as a land of plenty. Its agelong association with death and desolation is decisively erased as the poet presents a land of frenetic movement where even such forces of inertia as the rocks become violently mobile, and where the transformation of snow to ice is magnified to reveal frenzied process. The animated scene serves a function beyond the purely descriptive; nature's energy is a metaphor for the undescribed vigor of the Han troops in battle.

The conclusion is an interesting variation on the traditional "ellipsis of battle," for poetic convention joins historical fact: the battle is not described because it may not take place at all. "Jushi" (Karakhoja) contains a possible allusion to that tribe's faint-hearted king who had died of fright on the eve of meeting the Han army in battle in 638. Since General Feng and his troops have shown great ferocity and resolve, the poet surmises that his enemies too may be cowed into submission before the battle even takes place. Once more the poem concludes on a note of hyperbolic praise.

The extent of Cen Shen's originality in these war poems cannot become apparent without some knowledge of other frontier compositions. In making the frontier a vehicle for the expression of boundless energy, Cen overturns its traditional associations. The elegiac tone of the two well-known poems below is much more typical of the Chinese poetic response to the frontier and to war:

Ballad: Joining the Army in Antiquity
by Li Qi

Under a white sun I climb the mountain to scan
 the beacon fires.
At yellow dusk, I water my horse beside Jiaohe.
The traveler's gong dims in the windy sand;
The princess's piba fraught with silent
 grievance.
A barrack in the wilderness, a myriad miles
 without city walls.
Pell-mell, rain and snow join the great desert.
With plaintive cries, the Tartar goose night
 after night cries;
Tears from the Tartar lad, pair by pair, they
 flow.
Hearing that Jade Pass is again blocked,
I should pledge my life to expel the light
 carts.
Year by year battle bones buried in the
 wilderness beyond;
Vainly, the sight of grapes entering the Han
 house.[45] (1348)

Song: Upon the Frontier
by Wang Changling

Cicadas sing among the mulberry trees,
In the eighth month on the road to Xiao Pass.
Leaving the frontier, entering the frontier;
Yellow reed grass everywhere.
Always the retainers of You and Bing.
Grow old heading for the sandy battlefield.
Do not be a knight-errant lad,
And boast of your fine black stallion.[46]
(1420)

The occasion of Cen Shen's two poems limits his range of expression. The threnodic voice of lyric poetry such as we find in the Wang Changling and Li Qi poems is not appropriate in a composition wishing one's superior success. Yet Cen makes a virtue out of the necessity of the occasion, for the last two compositions must be considered two of the boldest and most vigorous war poems in Chinese. The desert is made into a compelling metaphor for man's warring spirit. In these poems Cen's demand for novel subject and startling diction is matched to an equally original and forceful vision of life. Scene and significance achieve perfect balance.

Feng Changqing's victorious return was greeted by Cen in a suite of six quatrains composed in yet another style which bears no resemblance to the two poems sending off the general:

64-69. Paeans: Presented to Lord Feng on his Victory over the Charchans
Heptasyllabic quatrains. Date: 754

The Han general received royal favor and crushes
  our foe in the west.
A swift dispatch of victory reported first at
  Weiyang Palace.
The emperor prepares to receive him at Unicorn
  Chamber.
Revering the past, who counts the merits of
  Ershi?[47]

Army carts leave westwards passing Loulan.
Tents encamped alongside "Moon Cavern" so chill.
The dawn frost of Rush Lake curdles our horses'
  tails;

Frontier Poetry

> The night snow of Scallion Mountain flutters over
> our flag pole.⁴⁸
>
> Singing pipes, beating drums envelop our returning
> troops.
> Such fall of states, such disarming of barbarians
> are unknown till now.
> My lord's magpie seal flutters under the frontier
> moon;
> My general's dragon flag tugs the lake's clouds.⁴⁹
>
> The sun sets behind the great gate, drums and horns
> sound;
> A thousand handcuffed faces emerge from the tribal
> citadel.
> We wash our arms at Fish Lake, clouds welcome our
> ranks;
> We graze our horses at Dragon Dunes, the moon shines
> over our camp.⁵⁰
>
> From afar the barbarian army looks on the
> Han barracks.
> Throughout the valleys, over the hills,
> the sound of weeping everywhere.
> Ten thousand arrows, a thousand daggers
> slaughter all night long;
> As dawn breaks, oozing blood soaks the
> empty citadel.
>
> Dusk rain upon flags and banners is not yet dried;
> Tartar dust over the white grass, the sunlight
> chills.
> Last night the general battled to dawn.
> In the tribal army, the sight of empty saddled
> horses. (2103)

These quatrains treat various aspects of Feng Changqing's campaign and victory; the first poem recounts the report of victory to a delighted emperor while the second describes the army on the march. The next two quatrains attend to the triumphant Han troops whereas the last two depict the vanquished enemy.

Martial feats here become the subjects of exquisite and elegant tableaux. With many stylishly matched couplets, the quatrains are reminiscent of early Tang poetry. Such antithetical couplets as "We wash our arms at Fish Lake, the clouds welcome our ranks, / We graze our horses on Dragon Dunes, the moon shines over our camp," take us back to the pageantry of the "Morning Audience at Daming Palace." The quatrain is generally considered to be too short to accommodate antithetical couplets comfortably. Yet Cen Shen uses this device to stunning effect in these quatrains.

We cannot be sure if the next quatrain dates to the period of Feng Changqing's campaign in 754. It offers a good example of Cen's stylistic range. The spare diction and narrow tonal range – all five words in the last line are in the level tone – are in striking contrast to the ornamentation of the last six quatrains.

70. Song: Extinguishing the Tartars
Pentasyllabic quatrain

The commander has extinguished the Tartars
 anew.
His men and horses – their spirit too is
 robust.
Dole and drear, the caitiff dust is cleared.
Bald and bare, Tianshan thrusts high.[51]
(2101)

Possibly this is Cen Shen's private and more sober voice when he is not under the constraint to sing of the renown of his general. From a personal point of view, Feng Changqing's triumph brought little sense of fulfillment as the following poem addressed to friends and colleagues indicates:

71. Ascending the Northern Loft Building of Beiting: Presented to the Various Gentlemen of the Camp
Pentasyllabic ancient style

I used to read in the chapter on the western
 region,
Of how the Han house obtained Luntai.
This ancient frontier, void for a
 thousand years;
Yin Mountain alone so cragged.
The two courts approach the West Lake.
In the sixth month the autumn wind arrives.
At dusk we climb the northern loft building.

An air of killing thickens and does not dispel.
In this wasteland no bird flies;
Only the sight of the white Dragon Dunes.
My beloved country infinitesimal at the sky's tip;
My homing heart each day more remote.
The great general again has smashed the Tartars;
In the outskirts of the citadel smoke and dust cease.
Within the frontier citadel all quiet, nothing to do;
We clasp our swords, vainly we pace to and fro.
T'is fortunate I've come to this camp,
And cast my lot with this group of talented men.
Long have I known a plan for pacifying the frontier,
I've yet to fulfill my life aspiration.[52]
(2024)

The opening couplet evokes the sagas of war and peace recounted in the official histories which Cen Shen had studied so assiduously in his youth. The following lines speak of emptiness and ennui, since the speaker has no part in the general's exploits. Indeed, his superior's success in pacifying the tribes merely increases his own sense of purposelessness. The conclusion is a sardonic comment on the opening lines, since the plan for bringing peace to the frontier which Cen had learned from his study of history has become superfluous. Yet it is ironical that the surrogate excitement of the campaign from which he is excluded, rather than the private lyric impulse, educed the most vigorous poetry from Cen Shen. In his frontier works, no less than in his nature poems, Cen's imagination thrives upon the realization of action.

Another group of poems attends to the persons of the commanders themselves. The following quatrain captures the bravura of a frontier general:

72. The Song of General Zhao
Heptasyllabic quatrain

On Tianshan in the ninth month, a wind like dagger.
Hunting horses north of the citadel shrivel

cold hairs.
The general wagers heavily and wins each round,
He gambles and wins the khan's sable coat. (2106)

Heroic exploits are represented not in battle, but in sports, as the general challenges his adversary to a game of chess (boyi). A correspondence between the human and natural world obtains here; the horses' hair shriveled in cold matches the khan's sable coat, and frigidity is correlated to hostility.

In a tour de force of exuberance, the next poem considers a frontier commander when he is not engaged on the battlefield. The general is probably Gai Tinglun, Cavalry Commissioner of Hexi, whom Cen visited on his way back to court in 756.

73. Song: General Gai of Jade Gate Pass
Irregular ancient style. Date: 756

General Gai,
What a man!
At thirty he is bearer of the golden apotropaion;
Seven foot tall with quite a beard.
The citadel of Jade Gate Pass is far and lone;
Yellow sand for a myriad miles, white grass
   withers.
Adjoining the Rong tribe in the south, neighboring
   the Hu Tartars in the north.
The general arrives, he prepares for sudden danger.
Five thousand armored troops, bold and brawny.
When there's no disturbance, there's only merry-
   making.
In a warm room, embroidered blinds and red
   braziers;
Patterned rugs woven as wall hangings.
Before the lamps, maid servants pour from jade
   flasks;
Gold vessels sparkle upon rustic delicacies.
Purple sashes and golden seals upon scurrying
   attendants;
Inquiring, we discover they are only veteran slaves.
A pair of lovely ladies demure and dainty;
Vermilion lips, kingfisher brows and bright glances.
They sing a clear song, the rarest on earth.
Today we rejoice to hear "The Phoenix Fledgling."
Lo, their loveliness surpasses Qin Lofu;

Frontier Poetry

The envoy's five horses shilly and shally.
The wild grass is "nest stitches" on their purple
  gossamer jackets;
The carved horses are red castanets facing the
  shupu dice.
Onto the jade plate, a slender hand casts the dice
  and gets all black;
The crowd roars, and says she cannot loose.
In your stables are all fine colts, so fleet;
A peach flowered Ferghana steed the most valuable
  of all.
Mounting it, you hunt south of the citadel;
On the day of the hunt, you shoot an ancient fox.
I come from beyond the frontier to examine the
  frontier granaries.
I'm drunk with your wine and there's wine to spare.
Drunken, we vie for the cup, we clamor and shout;
Suddenly we recall the old carousers of
  Xianyang.[53] (2058)

In the next poem Cen gives a spirited description of the horse of a military commander. Praise, perhaps, seems most sincere when it is least direct. In poetry, praise of the man is often displaced to his estate, to his horse, and to other indices of his character and taste. The horse as metaphor of the man is used by Du Fu in several compositions. In composing the following poem, Cen might have had some of Du's works in mind, most notably the "Protector General Gao's Piebald," dating to the early part of the 750s.

74. The Chestnut Charger of Regional Commander Wei
Heptasyllabic ancient style. Date: 759

Your chestnut charger cannot be painted.
A ball of cyclone, the color of peach.
Red bridle tassels, purple bridle, coral whip;
Jade studded saddle, damask bridle cloth, and
  yellow gold bit.

Please bring forth your armguard and let us see
  you ride.
Its tail is long, swishing the ground like red
  silk threads.
You boast that no horse can match this one;

As you recall the time you bought it for a
hundred gold pieces.

Within the scented streets and purple boulevards
of the phoenix city;
The spectators of the whole city look on, who
does not love it?
When the whip cracks, it dashes forth with white
sweat foaming;
When a shadow plays, it proudly advances, its
jasper hooves shattering.

A red bearded Tartar lad with gold shears,
At dawn shears the triple mane so tall.
Behold it in the stable, it alone is noble;
Lead it from the crowd, it is exceptionally bold.

Mounting it for the hunt at the mouth of the
south mountain;
The foxes and hares south of the city can no
longer be found.
A dot at the grass tip, fleet as if in flight;
It leaves the blue grey eagle lagging behind.

I recall seeing you recently at the Weiyang
audience.
Your clinking jade reins and enveloping canopy
scent the road.
I then know that frontier generals have real
fame, real fortune;
Lo, how radiant the man and the horse.

Every man wishes to be like this:
A noble steed whinnying as the north wind
rises,
Awaiting your departure from the east to sweep
the Tartar dust.
Galloping for you a thousand leagues each
day.[54] (2057)

These last two compositions depict the frivolous side of the
life of action. The world of war and punitive expeditions is
not totally forgotten, but it is foreshortened to a brief
acknowledgement. In the poem on General Gai, the long
section describing the festivities in the camp is preceded by

five lines (5-9) which state that the general has made such thorough preparations against the enemy that there is no longer any work left undone. The "Chestnut Charger" moves in the reverse order; beginning with an account of the magnificent trappings of the horse, the poem describes its beauty and its performance in the hunt. In the last two tetrastichs, horse and master leave to repel the barbarians.

Native readers ruled, almost instinctively at times, by the Ruist necessity of justifying literature in terms of didactic intent have proposed that Cen's exuberant depictions of these frontier commanders and their splendid life-style contain indirect criticism of the incontinence and excess that marred the last years of Xuanzong's reign. Perhaps it is all the more necessary to furnish such a justification in view of the fact that the two poems date to the beginning of the An Lushan uprising, an event which stirred Cen's friend Du Fu to such heights of moral outrage and impassioned poetry. Yet Cen's works seem to resist didactic interpretation. His childlike delight in the magnificence of the commanders seems at first reading to be unclouded by any concern for their wastefulness. His acknowledgement of the serious enterprise of war, no sooner made than glibly dismissed, tends to obliterate rather than clarify the moral ambiguity of this life-style. The distance between Cen's position and the Ruist stance is apparent if we compare Cen's last composition on the horse to Du Fu's poem dedicated, coincidentally, to Cen's erstwhile superior, Gao Xianzhi:

The Ballad of the Piebald of Protector General Gao

The Anxi protector-general's blue Kokonor piebald;
Its fame so brilliant spreads eastwards.
This horse in the battle array has no peer;
United with the man - one heart in one great deed.

The deed accomplished, magnanimous care attends it.
Buoyantly it comes from the distant flowing sand.
Its heroic demeanor has yet to submit to the stable's shelter;
Its fierce spirit thinks still of tactics on the battlefield.

Strong ankles, high hooves like hard iron;
A few stomps on Jiaohe, the ice splits.

> Splashes of five petals and cloud patches on its coat.
> After ten thousand miles, see the blood sweating breed.
>
> The stalwart lads of Chang'an dare not mount it.
> It passes like a flash of lightening, letting the whole city know;
> Were it to grow old in silk tassels,
> How is it to leave on the road from Horizontal Gate?[55]

The high seriousness of Du Fu's poem is established in the first tetrastich, where master and horse are identified by a shared dedication to a noble cause. The horse shows indomitable will in its refusal to accept the safe if ignoble course of life and the poem concludes with tragic overtones as the poet states the classical heroic choice to exchange a long life for a brief but glorious career. Traditional critics such as Shi Buhua choose Du Fu's weight to Cen Shen's ease: "Cen's lines describe the horse's ability, but Du Fu is able to bring out the higher level of the horse's virtue."[56] In all fairness to Cen, it should be said that his poem is not so much an unsuccessful imitation of Du Fu as an attempt to chart an entirely different course for himself. He strives for the startling and pointed description that captures the most elusive of movements. Lines such as "A ball of cyclone, the color of peach" or "A dot at the grass tip, fleet as if in flight" freeze motion, sealing the instant into the permanent world of poetry. Nor, indeed, should Cen's apparent flippancy be lightly dismissed. It is impossible to accept the following statement as totally sincere:

> I then know that frontier generals have real
>   fame, real fortune.
> Lo, how radiant the man and the horse.
> Every man wishes to be like this. . . .

The naiveté and guilelessness are as studied, perhaps, as his controversial comment to Du Fu that there is nothing to redress in Suzong's strife-ridden court (see poem 6). The tone is one of teasing irony. Cen is also aware of the moral compromises and social incongruities that inspired so much of Du Fu's poetry. He, however, prefers to express this awareness with breezy irreverence rather than

Frontier Poetry

impassioned rhetoric.
   Literary historians generally assign the waning of Tang frontier poetry to the years following the An Lushan rebellion when the grim reality of war eradicated any remaining illusions about military glory. Cen stopped writing about the frontier and about war shortly after his return to court in 757. In the remaining years of his life he was to witness numerous uprisings and to take part in at least two military expeditions. He never wrote about these late martial experiences with the exuberance of the years in Anxi and Beiting. One of his last poems was composed when he was stranded at the border of Rongzhou and Luzhou (modern Yibin, Sichuan) by a band of insurgents. The piece is almost indistinguishable from the scores of Chinese poems which depict war as wanton destruction:

75. Blocked by a Group of Bandits between Rong and Lu
   Pentasyllabic ancient style. Date: 768

In the year wushu (768), I left my office and
returned east. This poem was composed when
the river route was cut off and I tarried at
Rongzhou.

The jungles of the south are lush and deep;
Desperadoes gather within.
Slaughtering from dawn to dusk;
Piles of corpses fill the river bend.
Famished tigers pick on bones;
Starved crows peck on entrails.
A stench envelops the dead at the bank's grass.
Blood flows, turning the river crimson;
At night it rains, the wind swishing.
Ghosts wail throughout the mountains of Chu.
Upon the three rivers travelers are cut off;
For a thousand miles, not one journeying boat.
Only the white birds fly;
Emptily I see the autumn moon wax.
I left my post and started from southern Shu,
Taking the route to this river. . . . (2047)

If he could only find, Cen goes on to say, the magic wand that shrank distance and took Fei Changfang home. The poem concludes with the statement that troops had been dispatched to quell the rebels, but that, so far, they have had so little success that Cen could only fear for his life. The leader of the insurgence that cut off Cen's homeward route had revolted against his superior in much the same way that Gai Tinglun had taken up arms and killed his commander the year following Cen's effusive eulogy to him. But with a new victim's satiety for war, Cen now adopted the classical attitude and reverted to the conventional outlook of war poetry. The circle is complete. Beginning with the derivative nature poems in the mode of his great kaiyuan older contemporaries, Meng Haoran and Wang Wei, Cen tried brilliantly and daringly to work across the grain of poetic tradition, only to return to the grooves of common passage at the end.

Chapter Five
Evaluations
Critical Opinion during the Tang

In one of his few references to the art of poetry, Cen Shen praises a friend's compositions for their clarity (qing) and their novelty (xin), likening them to a "limpid lake whose myriad fathomed bed is visible to the eye," and "a patch of ice shining bright."[1] The critical term qing describes the elegant yet simple style, neither unduly intense nor weak, that is often associated with Xie Tiao (464-499) and later on with Meng Haoran. Xin, often appearing in combination with qi, the startling or strange, refers to freshness of diction and content. Cen might well have been speaking of his own poetic art in the above passage, for it has been felt both during his lifetime and afterward that clarity and newness are two distinguishing qualities of the Cen Shen style. Thus Du Fu claims that Cen has "many new poems,"[2] and that he "relishes the strange."[3] Writing on another occasion to both Gao Shi and Cen Shen, he inquires of the two: "Have you composed more verses, both clear and new?"[4] Du goes on to observe that Cen Shen and Gao Shi combine the merits of the early masters Shen Yue (441-513) and Bao Zhao (?-465): "You do not move with dilatory steps, / When the mood is right, mountain passes fly in movement."
  In his preface to Cen's works, Du Que reiterates Du Fu's earlier opinion; for Du Que, Cen's phrasing is both "noble and clear; his content has verity and relevance. His works must be included in the category of the excellent for they are distinguished by a unique elegance that differs from conventional sentiments." He goes on to note that Cen is often compared to Wu Yun (469-520) and He Sun (480-530), two poets of the Liang period and contemporaries of Shen Yue.
  The first compiler of Cen's works also attempted to place the poet within the context of the development of Tang poetry. He maintains that Cen is one of a dozen or more poets of the kaiyuan era who restored the orthodox and classical values to a poetry which had been dominated for the last two hundred years by the so-called "palace style"

111

(gongti). Developed during the Six Dynasties and widely popular through the early Tang, the palace style emphasizes phonic-timbric euphony and verbal ingenuity over substantiveness; pleasing, if occasionally fatuous, sentiment often replaces the search for essential truth. Du Que maintains that Cen and his contemporaries rejected the dominance of the Six Dynasties' style and revived the values of the ancient masters, most notably those of the revered Jian'an poets,[5] which traditional poetics consistently describe as "vigorous" (zhuang), "substantive" (shi), and "classical" (ya), as opposed to the palace style, which they generally characterize as "frivolous" (qingbo) and "gorgeously beautiful" (li).

Du Que also maintains that Cen's poetry was widely read in his time. "Even rustics and barbarians know and recite his works." This is a stock remark of compilers wishing to justify their own enterprise by maximizing the importance of their subjects. A more impartial indication of contemporary opinion may be gleaned from the anthologies compiled during the Tang itself. Of the ten extant collections dating from this period,[6] a sample of Cen's works appears in three, namely Yin Fan's Heyue yingling ji and two late Tang collections, Wei Zhuang's Youxuan ji (Another volume of profound works, preface dated 900) and Wei Hu's Caidiao ji (The works of talented literati). Compared with his contemporaries, Cen is not as well represented as Wang Wei and Gao Shi, who appear in five anthologies, or Wang Changling, Meng Haoran, and Li Qi, who are represented in four. However, he fares better than Du Fu and at least as well as Li Bo. That Tang taste differed significantly from later evaluations of its poetry is clear from the poor representation in contemporary anthologies of these two poets, acknowledged by later ages as the greatest of that dynasty. Li Bo's works are found in the same three anthologies as Cen's, and Du Fu is all but ignored, with seven entries in Wei Zhuang's collection. On the other hand, relatively minor poets such as Zu Yong (jinshi 724), Cui Hao, and others, who are now remembered only by a few popular anthology pieces, are generously represented.

Seven of Cen's poems are included in Yin Fan's Heyue yingling ji;[7] covering some twenty-four poets and 234 compositions, Yin Fan follows the format of Zhong Hong's (ca. 468 - ca. 518) Shipin (Classification of poetry) by furnishing a statement of evaluation for each poet. Although he does not formally use the Shipin's method of placing each

Evaluations 113

poet into one of three categories of excellence, his anthology too is divided into three parts. Cen appears at the beginning of Part B, following Li Bo, Wang Wei, Gao Shi, Li Qi, and others in Part A. Yin Fan's description of Cen Shen's poetic art converges with Du Fu's and Du Que's. "His diction is startling, his form, strong and energetic; his meaning also is startling." Yin singles out two couplets as representing Cen's art at its best: "A long wind blows the white rushes, / The wild fire burns dry mulberry leaves;" and a couplet from poem 32: "The mountain wind blows into the empty wood; / Swish-swishing as if someone were there." He commends the first pair of lines for its easy, unfettered quality and he claims that the second couplet captures the essence of the spirit of reclusion. Governed by a taste for expressions of remorse by frustrated literati, Yin Fan did not select from the frontier works for which Cen Shen is to become best known. The seven poems by Cen in the Heyue yingling ji are either bucolic pieces celebrating the life of retirement or songs about life's brevity that were inspired by the folk (yuefu) tradition.

Critical Opinion after the Tang

Interest in Cen Shen's poetry continues after the Tang. By the Ming dynasty, his place in the pantheon of major High Tang poets is widely acknowledged. Hu Zhenheng (fl. 1630)[8] places him among the celebrated figures of High Tang poetry. Gao Bing (1350-1423)[9] refers to Li Bo, Du Fu, Wang Changling, Gao Shi, Cen Shen, Li Qi, and Chang Jian as the "flowers of the flourishing Tang." Dividing the poets into several categories such as the pioneers, the great poets, the greatest poets, and those who made the transformations, Gao Bing places Cen among the great poets for his achievement in the pentasyllabic ancient and modern style, and among the pioneers for his contribution to the development of the heptasyllabic modern style.

Cen's defense of the classical poetic values continues to receive critical notice after the Tang. In the Song, Yan Yu repeats Du Que's contention that Cen contributed significantly to the revival of those ancient values epitomized by the Jian'an tradition. The term Yan uses to describe the works of Cen Shen and Gao Shi, "manly sorrow" (beizhuang),[10] is closely related to the term kangkai, that sense of strength in sorrow which Liu Xie (fl. 465), in his seminal work of literary criticism, the Wenxin diaolong (The carved dragon in the heart of literature),[11] had defined as the governing spirit of Jian'an poetry. Both Hu Zhenheng and Xin Wenfang (fl. 1304) observe that Cen's poetry is imbued with fenggu, "wind and bone,"[12] a term that defies precise translation since it covers a range of meanings. Generally speaking, feng refers to the power and vigor of a work while gu designates its inner substance and structure. While the meaning of the term may be open to interpretation, the type of poetry it describes is never unclear. Fenggu describes the classical tradition of which Han and late Han poetry are the paradigm. Hu Zhenheng also views Cen Shen as a successor of Chen Zi'ang (661-702), one of the first Tang poets to advocate an ancient revival and an ardent admirer of Jian'an poetics. Cen Shen, he claims, fuses spirit and substance (qigu) to Chen Zi'ang's ancient decorum (guya).[13]

Poetics after the Tang continue to recognize those qualities that had been singled out by his contemporaries as distinguishing marks of the Cen Shen style. The terms qing ("clear"), xin ("novel"), and qi ("extraordinary") recur in later discussions of his poetry and there are attempts to find specific examples of the ways in which Cen achieved these effects. In the main, these traditional critical comments cannot satisfy the modern reader, whose taste cannot be easily disengaged from New Criticism's emphasis upon poetic unity. Scholars like Yin Fan, interested in the technical problems attendant upon writing a poetic line or couplet, were ready to appreciate the strength of isolated lines irrespective of the merits of the whole poem.[14] Thus Xu Ju (Ming dynasty), remarking on the boldness of the pivotal fourth word of the heptasyllabic line (known as the "eye" of the line) in some Cen poems, cites the use of the word dian ("dot") in the following lines as examples of startling descriptions that elude the grooves of common linguistic passage; the lines describe a boat and a galloping horse, respectively: "Upon the rapids, a dot of lonely boat moon. . . " At the grass tip, a dot fleet as if in flight. . ."[15] Hong Liangji (1746-1809) notes that the startling effect should not be achieved at the expense of verisimilitude.[16] For him, Cen's poetry strikes a pleasing balance between the ordinary and the extraordinary in a manner that some of Li He's (791-817) works fail to do. As an example he cites the arresting couplet from poem 63 which renders an extraordinary scene plausible: "A river bank of loose rocks, large as bushel baskets, / Rushes with the wind, rolling all over the ground. . ." Shen Deqian[17] comments on Cen's mastery of the art of beginning a poem; pointing out the virtues of a strong initial couplet for the pentasyllabic regulated style poem, he offers, as illustrations, the first line of several Tang poems, including Cen's "I escort a guest beyond the flight of birds." Shen compares this line to "a rock tumbling from the mountain height. One does not know whence it comes but it is truly thrilling." He also commends the first line from poem 38 as being equally startling. Shi Buhua selects the couplet "The pavilion so high beyond the bird's flight, / The traveler's destination, far as the clouds;" as an example of the arresting first couplet.[18]

Native scholars continue to note the simple yet elegant clarity of Cen's poetic style. While Shi Buhua observes that the terse diction and fast pace of poem 63 effectively capture the urgency of the military combat,[19] Hu Zi compares the first couplet of poem 33, "At the ferry, it is almost dusk, / Home farers vying to cross, clamor;" favorably to Meng Haoran's celebrated "A bell chimes at the mountain temple, the day has turned to dusk, / At the ferry of Fisherman Bridge, by night vying to cross, they clamor." Hu considers Cen's couplet more spare in diction and more conclusive in meaning.[20]

Strength and vigor conjoined to invention make Cen Shen's style especially suited to poems about war and the unusual frontier landscape where the battles between the Han people and the nomadic tribes were customarily waged. This observation was made as early as the Song by Xu Yi: "Cen Shen's poetry is in a class by itself. He served in Feng Changqing's army and recorded copiously the extraordinary events of the western region."[21] In the course of the next centuries Cen became gradually known as the poet of the frontier. In the Qing, Shi Buhua maintains that his compositions are "vigorous and startling like an eagle in the frosty sky; his style lends itself especially well to frontier poems."[22]

The above survey of critical opinion of Cen Shen's art since the Tang shows a remarkable degree of accord. In describing his poetry, native scholars converge at two sets of literary terms that are associated with two disparate poetic traditions. "New," "startling," and "clear" belong to the poetic values of the Six Dynasties, while "manly sorrow," "vigorous spirit," and "substantiveness" describe the earlier, and what is generally deemed more orthodox, tradition of the

Han and late Han. The earlier poets mentioned as having molded Cen's poetic art conform also to this schema. Wu Yun, He Sun and Shen Yue are major poets of the Six Dynasties while Jian'an poetry, Chen Zi'ang, and even Bao Zhao[23] represent the classical tradition, revived during Cen's age in opposition to the palace style that was the vogue during the Six Dynasties.

Cen Shen's sympathies for the ideals represented by the Jian'an period are, as we have seen, widely noted. They accord with the spirit of his age. Thus his great contemporary Li Bo said with his characteristic bravura: "The classical airs have not been composed for so long; / Who but myself can now present them?"[24] Yin Fan in the mid-eighth century used fenggu as a criterion for the selection of works into the Heyue yingling ji. Cen Shen's commitment to the classical tradition thus reveals him as a man of the age. Literary historians like to proclaim this allegiance because it corresponds to their own periodization. His indebtedness to the Six Dynasties, while difficult to refute, is treated with considerable caution.

Traditional periodization of Tang poetry into three or four ages - Early, High, (Middle,) and Late - demands a complete break between Early and High Tang.[25] Cen, as a poet of the High Tang, should in theory have repudiated the residual palace style of the previous age. One must also remember that the Six Dynasties' values have always weighed heavily on the conscience of Chinese scholars nurtured on the belief in the moral and didactic ends of poetry. Consequently the legacy of the Six Dynasties upon Cen Shen has been given short shrift. Yet the poet's search for novelty and for arresting diction evokes a Six Dynasties' poetic concern; Liu Xie, for example, had spoken of the attempt of the writers of the Song period (420-477) to achieve the "startling in a single line and the novel in literary expressions."[26] Despite the tendency to minimize the influence of the palace style upon High Tang poetry, there is no doubt that the works of Cen Shen and his contemporaries involve more than a simple restoration of ancient values. The centuries that intervened between Jian'an and Tang gave poets an awareness of craftsmanship, a sensitivity for the purely aesthetic problems isolated from extraneous, nonliterary concerns. Cen Shen's discriminating use of words, noted by the numerous ancient scholars whom I quoted earlier, shows a sophistication that distinguishes his compositions from early poetry.

Du Que appears to have recognized the advances made

since the late Han, for he views the poetry of the kaiyuan period as a synthesis of the two disparate traditions which preceeded it. In his preface to Cen's works he describes the changes that have occurred in poetry: from the time of the Emperor Jianwen of Liang (503-551) and of Yu Xin (513-581), the emphasis upon the beautiful led to the development of the palace style. Throughout this period the classical ideals that had sustained poetry since the Shijing were discarded in favor of gorgeous verses. The notion that poetry should serve a political and didactic purpose (fengjian bixing) became unfashionable. Du Que observes that this temper ran its course and by the Tang the opposite taste reasserted itself. The plain and the unadorned (pu) became favored over the ornate and the taste for trifling prettiness subsided. Du goes on to say that some ten poets and more during the beginning of the kaiyuan era were able to join "the classical" with the "beautiful," to unify the ancient and the modern. This last comment indicates that Du Que regards the achievement of Cen Shen and his contemporaries as more than a revival of late Han poetic values, as, indeed, a feat of equilibrating and integrating the most enduring aspects of the divergent poetic stances. Yin Fan reiterates this view: "After 737, tonal euphony (whose rules were formulated by Shen Yue) and spirit and substance (the governing qualities of Jian'an poetry) have all reached perfection."

The reconciliation of the Six Dynasties and Jian'an was perhaps achieved more smoothly in the practice than in the theory of poetry. The divided theoretical loyalty of the High Tang poets reveals itself in a witty and equivocal quatrain by Du Fu:

In Jest

Not belittling the moderns loving the ancients;
Clever phrases and beautiful lines must be
  neighbors.
Secretly aspire towards Qu Yuan and Song Yu,
  fitting that they ride together;
Afraid with/compared to Qi Liang, dust behind.[27]
(2452)

Assuming that Du Fu is referring to his contemporaries in the "moderns," is he stating his preference for the works of the Six Dynasties by saying that he does not necessarily belittle the moderns' love of the ancients but that clear phrases and beautiful lines (the qualities associated with the Qi and Liang as well as the early Tang) must be his neighbors? It is equally possible that he is saying that he favors the ancients: "I don't belittle the moderns but I love the ancients, for in their works clear phrases and beautiful lines too are neighbors." Then perhaps Du is suggesting that a fusion is possible; "I don't belittle the moderns or love the ancients; clear phrases and beautiful lines are neighbors in any period." The fourth line is equally ambiguous. Is Du Fu denigrating Qi and Liang by saying that he is afraid of lagging behind the ancients with (yu) the Qi Liang poets? Or does he use yu as an expression of comparison and is saying that he and his age lag behind when their achievement is compared to that of the Six Dynasties' masters?

Whatever theoretical difficulties Cen and his contemporaries might have encountered, this did not deter them from learning from the different traditions. As Du Que points out, it is Cen's ability to combine the antipodal if equally vital qualities of decorum and beauty which takes his works to new heights of achievement. In the Ming, an even greater Cen Shen devotee went so far as to place his gift for synthesis above that of Du Fu and Li Bo. Bian Gong (1476-1532) in the colophon to the Ming edition of Cen's poetry writes: "Energy and ease, the startling, the sorrowful and the strong – Du Fu and Li Bo were unable to combine these virtues, yet Cen's works come close to achieving such a fusion."[28]

Most Chinese literary scholars demur at Bian Gong's evaluation, the general opinion being that Cen Shen is a great poet whose achievement is yet eclipsed by his greater contemporaries. Above all else, they question Cen's success in striking that delicate balance between the demands of art and of essential truth, in reconciling Jian'an and Six Dynasties. Traditional critical comments converge at the conclusion that Cen sometimes uses startling observations and lines of great felicity to compensate for lapses from truth and sincerity; hence his compositions often achieve distinction by isolated lines of great power rather than by integrality of vision. Lu Shiyong observes that he shows a "penchant for clever (qiao) lines which replaces truth (zhen)."[29] Comparing Cen Shen with Gao Shi, Hu Zhenheng maintains that in Cen's poetry "expression exceeds meaning; the lines are strong and beautiful but the spirit does not move."[30] He goes on to claim that Cen's works are always cleanly executed but lack "far reaching rhythm" or "resonance." In both forms of modern-style poetry, Cen shows a "talent for beautiful verse and a deficiency of real feeling."[31] Ye Xie (1627-1703) notes that Cen's heptasyllabic ancient-style poems contain some excellent lines but lack a sense of unity. He also observes that from the beginning to the concluding lines, there is little variation.[32]

Cen's sternest critics are offended by his mannerism, that is, his affected and excessive use of a single style. They find a wearisome sameness about a Cen Shen poem. Wang Shizhen (1526-1590) maintains that the poetic expressions of Li Yi (748-827) and Cen Shen are limited in range. "In structure and sentiment, most of their poems repeat each other."[33] As an example Ye Xie cites the following lines, which convey a commonplace sentiment through a series of well-worn images:

> In the morning when you climb Sword Peak,
>   the clouds follow your horses;
> At eve when you cross Ba River, the rain
>   washes your arms.
> Mountain flowers, a myriad buds welcome
>   your ongoing carriage;
> River willows, a thousand strands brush
>   your departing flags. . . .[34]

Such verse, Ye maintains, has an invidious effect upon later poetry for it supplies uninspired poetasters with a trove of facile observations and stock expressions. This is the harshest judgment passed upon Cen Shen in Chinese literary criticism. The poet does not lack apologists. Wang Shimao (1536-1588) observes that great Tang poets such as Wang Wei and Cen Shen can indeed be faulted for occasional lapses from restraint. Yet he finds a unique beauty and appeal even in the flawed passages.[35]

Chinese literary commentators thus seem agreed in the fact that Cen's works contain sections of great power and astonishing observation. They are only a little less unanimous in suggesting that the poet falls short of two of the enabling postulates of Chinese poetry; first, the idea that is Taoist in inspiration that great art should be disguised in artlessness. Cen's original diction and startling power of observation reveal rather than conceal consummate artistry. Hand in hand with the demand for spontaneity, is the emphasis upon resonance, that inferential and suggestive quality that allows the sentiment evoked by the poem to linger and resonate long after the act of reading has ended. The enforced brevity of modern style poetry encouraged the development of a style that depends upon the power of suggestion rather than of full description. Cen's style is deficient in this quality. Those very strengths for which he has been extolled, the arresting beginning noted by Shi Buhua and Shen Deqian, the air of finality observed by Hu Zi, and the originality that has impressed countless readers, undercut his ability to achieve the sense of rippling and far-reaching evocativeness which became increasingly valued from the Tang. Cen Shen's style is marked by clarity rather than ineffableness. The impact of his poetry is instantaneous rather than lingering.

The insights into Cen's limitations suggest that traditional literary criticism views him as being visited by the sins of the Six Dynasties. Even though his poetry cannot be mistaken for the works of the earlier era, Cen's impulse to achieve novelty underlines an aesthetic norm that derives from the Six Dynasties. His shortcomings are those inherent in this norm. Liu Xie had judged some of Six Dynasties' poetry in terms that might have guided the critics of Cen Shen. He finds the early Song period

> pretentious and novel; from substance, poetry moved to affectation; as it approached the present, it became increasingly paltry. Why is this? Because poets vie to be modern, they eschew the ancient values; the spirit is consequently lulled, vitality sapped.[36]

In the Fenggu section, he writes:

> If, before the substance and diction are fully realized and the spirit fully forged, a writer neglects old rules to pursue originality, he might indeed come up with some clever ideas but he would fail. Mere startling phrases cannot be mistaken for canonical principles. Thus the Book of Zhou states, "In writing one must emphasize the essential and not indulge in the startling."[37]

Gao Shi and Cen Shen

Our summary of traditional responses to Cen Shen's poetry cannot be complete without a discussion of a topic which may not readily suggest itself to scholars outside the native tradition but which is of sustained interest to Chinese scholars; this is the pairing of Cen Shen with his contemporary Gao Shi. Such well-known duos as Wang Wei and Meng Haoran, Li Bo and Du Fu, and Han Yu and Meng Jiao indicate that the pairing of poets for the purposes of critical discussion is a popular strategy in traditional poetics. The origin of this practice might be found in the peculiar circumstances which gave rise to so many poems. Verse was often a medium of communication between friends. The verses exchanged between Su Wu and Li Ling (d. 74 B.C.) joined these two men forever in literary history and might have begun a procedure that endures to the present. The practice gradually dissociated itself from biographical and historical reality to become a strategy of literary criticism.[38] In the case of Cen Shen and Gao Shi, there seems to be little biographical ground to link the two together. It is true that they were contemporaries who moved in the same circles in Chang'an. We know from the poems composed at the Temple of Compassionate Mercy that Gao had invited Cen and three other literati to join him for an excursion to that shrine. Other than the poems composed on such public occasions,[39] there is little in the two men's extant works to indicate intimate friendship. From the numerous verses presented to Du Fu by both of them, we gather they were better friends with Du than with each other. It was also Du Fu, in the previously mentioned poem sent to both Gao and Cen, who first associated them as a literary pair.

If there seems to be little biographical justification for discussing Cen Shen in unison with Gao Shi, there is some reason to consider them together in literary history. The two shared a common experience of serving as civilian officials in the armies of powerful military commanders. Both chose to make this experience the subject of some of their most ambitious works. Writing in the prime years of the High Tang, both men wanted to recover the classical values of poetry. Yan Yu was one of the first scholars to note this common interest. Following Yan, the two poets' emulation of the ancients is affirmed by a multitude of scholars including Hu Zhenheng, Gao Bing, Xin Wenfang, and Shen Deqian.[40]

Beyond the common interest in retrieving the principles of Han and late Han poetry and in writing of the frontier, the poetic tempers of the two men show significant differences. The critical attempts to distinguish the art of Gao Shi from that of Cen Shen reinforce the general evaluation of Cen. Consistently literary scholars find Gao to be more orthodox and classical while Cen is the original and consummate poet. Wang Shizhen writes that Gao Shi and Cen Shen are equally talented but that their poetry is clearly distinguishable; in spirit and substance Cen must defer to Gao while in elegance and vigor he is clearly the superior. Wang goes on to note that Cen is known for fast-paced ballads that are truly startling; Gao, on the other hand, tends to abide by conventions and is more orthodox.[41] Hu Zhenheng observes that Gao Shi's pentasyllabic ancient-style poems are subtle and complete even when there are occasional phonic-timbric flaws. For Hu, Cen's works are novel and limpid, startling and untrammeled; he is a great poet who epitomizes the High Tang achievement while Gao's plain and bland style captures the sense of antiquity (guyi).[42] Hu Yinglin expresses essentially the same opinion when he maintains that Gao Shi's strength lies in conveying the inner principle or idea (li), whereas Cen excels in depicting the external scene (jing);[43] Weng Fanggang claims that the former's works are distinguished by their matter and the latter's by their verbal cunning.[44] Commenting in a negative vein, Hu Zhenheng notes that in Gao's works meaning supersedes expression. The sentiments are intricate and subtle but the composition is often not equal to the emotion. Cen Shen suffers from the opposite defect; in his poems expression frequently exceeds meaning for the "lines and structure are strong and beautiful but the spirit fails to move."[45] On the whole, native critics seem to rank Gao Shi's orthodox approach above Cen's original achievement. Ye Xie states without reservation that Gao is a somewhat better poet than Cen.[46]

The Traditional Response Reevaluated

The insights of the native scholars mentioned in the previous sections are expressed in the seemingly casual and impressionistic manner typical of the "Talks on Poetry" (shihua). Unlike modern western criticism, the authors of these "Talks" do not submit their statements to the test of technical analysis or logical argumentation. This approach avoids one of the inherent paradoxes of contemporary criticism where one discerns a gap between criticism as a cognitive process and poetry's unique capacity to give us an

Evaluations 123

experiential grasp of our world, one which cannot be contained within a systematized, cognitive discipline. Eluding the order-imposing intellect, the poetic vision must also remain to some degree inviolate to the critic's discourse; for his methodology tends to lapse into a sort of scientism and, doing so, betrays an alien perspective. On the other hand, the Chinese exemption from this paradox is achieved at a price. Its procedure is, perhaps, most convincing in a society of shared experience and compatible sympathies. In the modern world of diverse values, the elliptical, nay cryptic, remarks of the "Talks on Poetry" confuse as often as they elucidate. The modern reader will often remain unconvinced by the views expressed in traditional Chinese literary criticism until they are verified by practical criticism of specific works. In the following pages, therefore, I will discuss some examples of Cen Shen's poetry and one of Gao Shi's specifically to test the validity of the traditional response to Cen Shen's art.

76. At Guozhou's East Pavilion in Late Spring, I Bid Farewell to Marshall Li Returning to His Retreat at Fufeng
Heptasyllabic regulated style. Date: 759-62

Willows catkins pendulate, orioles so coy, the
  flowers are crimson;
At the red pavilion with green wine, I escort
  you on your return.
You came here to Hangu's moon in sorrow;
You return there to Pan Creek's Mountain of
  your dreams.
Spring hues before the curtains must be
  treasured;
The floating fame of the mundane world is
  commonplace.
I gaze west to my homeland pass, my entrails
  about to snap;
Facing you with shirt sleeves streaked by
  tears. (2097)

Parting from Administrator Wei by Night
by Gao Shi

A high hall, tall lamps, the wine is clear;
A night bell, waning moon, sound of geese

homing.
T'is only said that the chirping bird takes
on the search for a mate;
Hapless, alas, the spring wind escorting you
in parting.
At Yellow River's bend, the sand forms a bank;
By White Horse Ford, the willows lean towards
the citadel.
Don't complain that you must leave for another
place;
I know you will find welcome wherever you go.
(2232)

These two heptasyllabic regulated poems are farewell verses to friends, leaving a provincial post for home in Cen Shen's case and departing for another region in Gao's. The formulae for the poetry of parting are amply represented in these two compositions; both begin with a reference to the farewell banquet. The second and third couplets in both pieces allude to the points of departure and destination. The conclusions, expressing grief and consolation, respectively, are also typical of this body of verse.

The first couplets of the two poems seem almost interchangeable. Both attend to the elegant farewell banquet in introductory lines of similar paratactical construction. The effect of the two couplets, however, is distinct. Cen Shen evokes a scene both sumptuous and exquisite. The reference to three vibrant and complementary colors, the words "coy" (jiao), and the recondite duo ("pendulate"), rather than the more common chui ("droop") all create a courtly atmosphere redolent of palace-style verse. Gao's initial lines, on the other hand, convey a totally different impression; "high hall" and "tall lamps" evoke a stately yet restrained world while "night bell" and "waning moon" are more evocative of a rustic than a courtly setting.

Gao Shi's first couplet ends with a reference to the wild goose, traditionally associated with autumn and also with letter-carrying; it is, therefore, a stock image in poems about traveling and parting. The wild goose makes a graceful transition to the next couplet and another avian image; the "chirping bird searching for its mate" is an allusion to poem 165 of the Shijing, which celebrates the duties and value of friendship. Then the fourth line amplifies another quality associated with the wild goose by means of a contrast. The bird is said to fly homeward in autumn. Here, however, the poet speaks of spring and remarks on the incongruity of saying sad farewell in this season of rejoicing. The last two words of the fourth line, "escort you in parting" (songxing), make the transition to the third couplet as adroitly as "wild goose" had shifted the first couplet to the second. The third pair of lines then evokes two places on the itinerary of the traveler and the poem concludes with an exhortation. Do not, Gao Shi tells the traveler, begrudge the fact that you must leave for a short time for you will find friends wherever you go. The source of comfort presented to the traveler is one which is denied to the poet and those friends who remain behind. If the departing friend can find distraction in fresh scenes and new acquaintances, the poet himself cannot look forward to such relief. The lovely season and scene evoked in the third couplet with its harmony of pastel colors reinforce the sense of pleasant expectancy. No such pleasure compensates for the poet's loss. His desolation is no less compelling because it is unarticulated, for reticence is sometimes more forceful than eloquence. Restraint concludes this dignified poem on a note of noble fortitude. The dominant tone is one of sorrow but also of strength. Gao Shi's restraint is not shared by Cen Shen, whose poem concludes with expressions of unconcealed grief. Like Gao, Cen juxtaposes the traveler's situation with his own in an effort to heighten the poignancy of his lot. Unlike Gao, his grief is strongly stated.

Following the exquisitely wrought first couplet, Cen continues to display his verbal flair in the second pair of lines, which is regarded as very original.[47] They are startling in their dislocation of normal grammatical order. A word-for-word translation would yield the following lines: "Come here Hangu sorrow midst moon / Go there Pan Creek dream in mountain." Dislocation of syntax and fluidity of parts of speech characterize poetic grammar and distinguish it from prose. The adjectival use of proper nouns is a common syntactical pattern in poetry. In this couplet, Cen extends that pattern by suspending the topic of each line (mountain and moon) to the end and by qualifying it with two sets of place words – the proper names (Hangu and Pan Creek) and the locative "midst sorrow" and "in dreams." Pan Creek, located near Marshall Li's retreat at Fufeng (modern Fengxiang, Shaanxi), is the place where Lu Shang, better known as Taigong Wang, the friend and companion of King Wen of Zhou, once fished. The allusion is appropriate because Marshall Li is returning to a life of retirement. At the same time Cen may be implying that like Taigong Wang, Marshall Li will continue to enjoy the sovereign's confidence and will ultimately be summoned out of reclusion. The tortuousness of Cen's second couplet is an interesting foil to the simplicity and colloquial plainness of Gao Shi's counterpart couplet. Beginning with a particle, zhi ("only"), and an exclamatory, wuna ("hapless, alas"), respectively, the lines have the natural rhythm of speech. Even though line 3 contains a poetic allusion, the couplet itself is as unforced as ordinary discourse.

Cen begins his third couplet by hearkening back to the beginning. "Before the curtains" returns to the scene of the banquet at the red pavilion. "Spring hues" have already been anticipated by the flowers and willows of the first couplet. Here in line 5 Cen gives a metaphoric extension to the season; the springtime of life is all too brief and fame is consequently worthless. Having said this much, the poet deprives himself of a reason to stay away from home and to continue in his official duties at alien Guozhou. The last pair of lines attends to his frustration and grief with such stock poetic expressions as "entrails about to snap" and "shirt sleeves streaked by tears." The reader realizes that the sadness engendered by the "moon over the pass" is a shared experience among the group of officials at Guozhou. Whereas Marshall Li has a reprieve and returns home, the poet does not share his good fortunes.

The reader is at first beguiled by Cen's brilliant and daring manipulations of language. His verbal dexterity startles and excites us in a way that Gao Shi's restrained diction fails to do. Yet even the most bedazzled of Cen's readers will admit that his poem is a fitful and uneven performance. Compared to the verve displayed in the first two couplets, the concluding lines fall back upon some very hackneyed expressions. Nowhere in Gao Shi's poem is there the verbal ingenuity of Cen's initial couplets. After reading Cen's composition, Gao's diction seems bland and his imagery, formulaic. Yet the totality of his vision transcends the sum of its parts. The interaction among the four couplets makes a complex statement about the experience of loss. Gao Shi manages to evoke a subtle mood that wavers between debilitating grief and indomitable strength. Intimating despair with words of optimism, introducing spring to images of autumn, he conveys human experience in all its complexity and inconsistencies. The simplicity, therefore, is only on the surface. Within the context of the whole poem blandness becomes noble restraint and the stock images are invested with new meaning. Cen Shen's farewell to Marshall Li lacks this maturity and integrality of vision. After the scintillating first couplets, the lines are disappointing. Moreover the sumptuous atmosphere conjured up by the first couplet hardly prepares the reader for the injunction to view wordly fame as commonplace. Consequently, the deprecation of official life lacks conviction. The traditional view that Cen's poetry is exquisite, if sometimes deficient in depth of feeling, and that, despite the beauty of isolated lines, it often lacks unity seems justified on the basis of the poem to Marshall Li.

Cen Shen would have no place among the major Tang poets if he were merely capable of turning out occasional deft lines within indifferent poems. At his best as in the following poem, Cen can bring his considerable poetic skill to the service of a vital spirit and a compelling vision of life. The composition attends to a popular subject of Tang poetry; the instructions left by Cao Cao, the King of Wei (155-220), that he be buried in a mound just northwest of his capital of Ye (modern Linchang, Henan); his entertainers were to be housed in the Copper Bird Tower, also known as Overlook Mound Tower, where a couch was to be reserved for himself.[48] The episode appears in poetry as a poignant reminder of an indomitable man's quest for immortal fame and of the futility of his grandiose designs. The ruins of Ye could still be seen during the Tang and Cen Shen's poem is a description of the abandoned city. He refers to Cao Cao as the "Martial Emperor" (Wudi) only once in the penultimate line. Cao's instructions, however, pervade every line:

77. Ascending the Ancient City of Ye
Irregular ancient style

I dismount and climb the citadel of Ye.
The city is empty, what is there to see?
The east wind blows a wild fire;
At dusk it enters Flying Cloud Chamber.
The city's corner to the south faces
  Overlook Mound Tower;
The waters of the Zhang to the east flow
  and do not return.
In the Martial Emperor's palace, all is
  gone.
Year by year, for whom do spring hues

come? (2061)

The description of ruins as an illustration of human ephemerality and vanity is, of course, an important topos of poetic contemplations of the past. The first two lines begin the poem in a matter-of-fact tone that leads the reader to anticipate a doleful contemplation of silence and stillness. He is, however, to be surprised by the dynamism and violent movement of the following lines. To the reader familiar with Chinese history, the east wind which fans the wild fire may stir memories of one of the most celebrated episodes in Cao Cao's illustrious military career; his defeat by Zhou Yu at Red Cliff. Sun Quan and Zhou Yu of the state of Wu had resorted to a bold ruse in their attempt to meet Cao's superior force. Availing themselves of the east wind, they had sent empty boats filled with straw to the northern banks of the Yangzi, where Cao's navy was anchored. The Wu army then shot fiery arrows at the unmanned flotilla once it reached the north bank; the fire on the flotilla spread to Cao's fleet, thereby destroying it.[49]

The east wind also refers to the spring wind and in poetry it often serves as a male sexual image.[50] The standard literary dictionaries cite the name Flying Cloud Chamber only in reference to this line by Cen Shen, which suggests that it is an obscure name. Cen's choice of this recondite name might well have been dictated by a desire to evoke the cloud, a female sexual image in Chinese poetry.[51] The undertone of erotic love comes to the surface in the last two lines; the palace attendants of the Martial Emperor are now all dead and gone; why do the colors of spring, lovely as the palace ladies' faces, bloom still with the season? Lines 3 and 4 thus operate on two levels; on the literal, representational level, they address themselves to the present desolation, but on the allusive and inferential level, they remind us of the past and a man of passion and grandiose vision, a great warrior and a romantic hero.

The following lines (5-6) are marked by a change of meter, from five to seven syllables. The elongated lines attend to wide-ranging space and extended time. In stating that space spans from the city's southern corner to the mound (in the northwest), thence to the Zhang River flowing easterly, the poem names two directions and alludes to the other two. Space often serves as a marker for time in poetry and the river's flow represents time's irretrievable passage. Lines 5 and 6 also evoke another aspect of the

Evaluations

central historical figure; because a sovereign traditionally was seated with his face to the south on public occasions, the epithet "south visage" (<u>nanmian</u>) is an antonomasia for the emperor. Cen's "south facing" (<u>nandui</u>) reminds the reader of the figure and consequently of the imperial Cao Cao. After the warrior and the lover, Cen invites us to remember the royal king.

The poem thus expresses one viewpoint, but, by verbal legerdemain, it conjures up opposite perspectives. Cao Cao's death and the annihilation of his empire are real to the physical eye. The poetic eye, however, sees beyond to a man most vital, passionate, and royal. The two points of view may seem mutually exclusive but the poet can, for the duration of the poem, sustain both views and in doing so, present experience in all its contradictory fullness. Such a composition invites comparison with the most vigorous work of any age.

Contemporary Critical Strategies

In the Tang, Yin Fan had praised Cen's poetry for capturing the essence of reclusion and in the Yuan dynasty, when Xin Wenfang spoke of his frontier poems, he did not neglect the poet's other achievements: "His works give expression to his feelings for mountains and woods. He cherished thoughts of retirement and composed arresting poems of reclusion." Modern critics, with their interest in theme rather than style, have concentrated almost without exception upon Cen's outstanding thematic contribution to Chinese poetry, namely his poems on the frontier.[52] Cen is now seen as the bard of the wars that marked Tang expansionism at its heights and of the alien regions beyond the Chinese empire. The authors of two of the recent standard histories of Chinese poetry divide the poetry of the <u>kaiyuan</u> and <u>tianbao</u> eras into two opposing schools; the first, represented by the works of Wang Wei and Meng Haoran, is described as the dispassionate expressions of the eremite whereas the later, represented by Gao Shi and Cen Shen, is the poetry of action and worldly commitment. The versatility of the great Tang poets is thus frozen into this neat dichotomy. The court poems of Wang Wei and the nature poetry of Cen Shen tend to be dismissed because they fail to fit into the present critical schema.

Contemporary criticism continues to discuss Gao Shi in conjunction with Cen Shen. Here too opinion seems to have reversed itself. Whereas Gao had been considered the better poet by virtue of his classicism, the iconoclastic modern age favors Cen precisely because of his originality and defiance of tradition. Lu Kanru and Feng Yuanjun state unequivocally that Cen is the more significant poet. Numerous studies of Cen Shen have appeared in Chinese and Japanese in recent years while Gao Shi languishes in comparative critical neglect.[53] Most recently, Stephen Owen, in his study of the great age of Tang poetry, treats the essential difference between the two poets as one of time; he considers Gao Shi as belonging to an earlier generation of poets than Cen Shen, whom he calls a poet of the tianbao era. The efforts of this second generation of High Tang poets to surpass the great achievement of their predecessors in the kaiyuan are revealed by a tendency toward excess of content and style. Owen views Cen Shen as the "overreacher" and a master of the flamboyant tianbao style whereas Gao is a classical and intellectual master of the more restrained previous generation.[54]

The selection from Cen Shen's poetic works in this study is made on the basis of their contribution to our understanding of the critical responses, both ancient and modern, to his poetry as well as to aspects of the poet's art which may suggest new evaluations.

Abbreviations Used in Notes and References and Bibliography

CSJC	Congshu jicheng edition.
Martin	Index to the Ho Collection of the Twenty-Eight shihua, ed. Helmut Martin (Taipei: Chinese Material Center, 1973).
QSH	Qing shihua (Poetry talks of the Qing dynasty), by Wang Fuzhi (1619-1692) et al. (Shanghai: Zhonghua Shuju, 1963).
QTS	Quan Tangshi (Complete poetry of the Tang), comp. Cao Yin (1658-1712) et al. (Beijing: Zhonghua, 1960).
QTW	Quan Tangwen (Complete prose works of the Tang), comp. Dong Gao (1740-1818) et al. (Taipei: Huawen Shuji, 1961).
SBCK	Sibu congkan edition.
SBBY	Sibu beiyao edition.
TCZZ	Tang Caizi zhuan (Biographies of the genius of the Tang dynasty), compiled by Xin Wenfang (fl. 1304) (Taipei: Shijie Shuju, 1960).
XLDSH	Lidai shihua xubian (Poetry talks of the successive ages: sequel), comp. Ding Fubao (reprinted Taipei: Yiwen, n.d.).
WX	Zhaoming wenxuan (Prince Zhaoming's anthology of literature), by Xiao Tong (501-531) (Taipei: Wenhua tushu gongsi 1971).
YFSJ	Yuefu shiji (Collection of Yuefu songs), comp. Guo Maoqian (ca. 1100); SBCK edition.

Unless otherwise noted, the Standard Dynastic Histories are cited in the punctuated texts published by Zhonghua shuju, Beijing. The following abbreviations are used:

JTS   Jiu Tangshu (Old history of the Tang),

by Liu Xu (887-946) et al., 1975.
XTS Xin Tangshu (New history of the Tang), by Ouyang Xiu (1007-72) et al., 1975.

Notes and References

References to older Chinese texts (or a modern reprint of an older text) are represented by two sets of numbers separated by a virgule. The first figure refers to the juan or fascicle number; the second, the page number. When the letters "a" and "b" appear after the second number, they refer to recto and verso, respectively. References to the QTS are represented by two numbers; the first refers to the page and the second to the serial number of the poem within the page.

Chapter One
1. QTW 358/4597.
2. The biographies of Cen Wenben, Cen Changqian, and Cen Xi are in JTS 70/2535-41 and XTS 102/3565-69.
3. Cen Shen's birth cannot be dated with complete certainty. His own references to his age in the poems are always in round numbers of thirty and forty. A poem written when he was appointed to his first post in 744 (QTS 2089/2) states that he was then thirty. Based on this reference, Wen Yiduo, in "Cen Jiazhou xinian kaozheng" (Textual evidence for Cen Jiazhou's chronological biography), in Complete Works (Shanghai, 1938), 3:119, places the poet's birth at 715. Other scholars (see Bibliography) place it at 714 and 718.
4. See note 1.
5. See QTS 2261/2, 1428/2, and 1509/3.
6. See note 1.
7. See QTS 2023/2 and 2040/4 for examples of these early eremitic poems.
8. XTS 123/4374.
9. QTS 1243/3.
10. In the fu "Moved by Past Events" (see note 1), Cen Shen writes: "At twenty I submitted my works to the imperial city." For the custom of submitting samples of works in lieu of taking the examinations, see the Fengshi wenjian ji (What Mr. Feng saw and heard), by Feng Yan (CSJC ed.), 3/2b. Examples of works used for this purpose are found among Quan Deyu's works in QTW 483/6245.
11. There is a poem addressed to his wife while traveling in the vicinity of Yongle in modern Henan (see QTS 2089/4).

Since Yongle was renamed Mancheng in 742, this would mean that Cen was already married by that year.

12. QTS 2031/3 and 2032/2.
13. See note 1.
14. Gaoguan "High Crest" in the title refers to a body of water on Mt. Zhongnan where Cen had a retreat. See poem 19.
15. The dating for Du Fu's Meipi poem is inconclusive since Cen Shen and Du Fu also saw each other in Chang'an in subsequent years. I follow the dating of William Hung, Tu Fu: China's Greatest Poet (Cambridge, Mass., 1952), p. 53, who feels that the tone of Du Fu's composition is that of an early work written on a first visit to the lake. Both Du and Cen left several poems on Lake Meipi. Lantian (line 20) refers to the district and mountain southeast of Chang'an. Fengyi (line 22) is the god of the waters and is better known as Hebo. "Ladies of the Xiang" refer to the consorts of the legendary emperor Shun who drowned in the Xiang River after Shun's death while the "maiden of the Han" is the guardian spirit of the Han River.
16. Gao Xianzhi was also in Chang'an the previous year (748). A poem written in farewell to Yan Zhenqing on his departure for Helong in 749 (see poem 55) indicates that Cen did not leave with Gao on the earlier date. Gao Xianzhi's biography is in JTS 104/3203-7 and XTS 135/4576-79.
17. QTS 2056/3.
18. The Long Mountain range stretches from Long, Shaanxi to Gansu, forming a natural barrier for western China.
19. In the preface to the "Song of the Youbenluo Flower" (QTS 2062/2), Cen writes that he was Assistant Commissioner of Public Revenue (duzhi fushi); this is probably a scribal error in which the first two characters were reversed, for junior revenue officers to regional commanders were known as zhidu fushi or Assistant Commissioner of Expenses.
20. Feng Changoing's biography is in JTS 104/3207-11 and in XTS 135/4579-81.
21. QTS 2090/1.
22. QTS 2090/5.
23. See note 19.
24. QTW 359/4621.
25. For Wuling, "The Five Mounds," see note 24, Chapter 4. Xianyang (line 13) is the name of an ancient city northwest of Chang'an; in the course of the centuries it was also known as Xincheng and Weicheng. Feng (line 16),

located east of Hu, Shaanxi, and Hao, southwest of modern Tang, Shaanxi, were the seats of government of the Zhou dynasty. All three names refer to the vicinity of the Tang western capital.

26. Gao Shi became regional commander of Huainan for a brief period in 757. Later on he held the military governorship of Jiannan and Xichuan and was eventually enfeoffed Marquis of Bohai. His biography is in JTS 111/3328, XTS 143/4679.

27. The Secretariat was known as the Purple Myrtle Office because this plant decorated its grounds.

28. See Huang Che (Song dynasty), Kongqi shihua (Kongqi's comments on poetry), 1/2/b, in XLDSH, vol. 2; Hu Zhenheng (fl. 1630), Tangyin guiqian (Examining the tenth stem of Tang sounds) (Shanghai: Zhonghua, 1959), 11/96; Xie Zhen (1495-1575), Siming shihua (Siming's comments on poetry), 4/1, in XLDSH, vol. 4.

29. QTS 2100/5.

30. Hung, Tu Fu, p. 124, and A.R. Davis, Tu Fu (New York: Twayne Publishers, 1971), p. 61.

31. Solar Floriate (Rihua) Gate was the eastern gate of the Xuanzheng Chamber, leading to the Chancellery. The matching gate to the Secretariat, known as Lunar Floriate (yuehua), was located at the western end of the Xuanzheng Chamber. Because of its position in relation to the great council chamber, the Secretariat was also known as the West Wing or Right Department whereas the Chancellery was known as the Left Department or East Wing.

32. See note 31.

33. Cen refers to this appointment in QTS 2100/5. Du Que claims that he was appointed Secretary of Activity and Repose (qiju lang) rather than Chamberlain of Activity and Repose (qiju sheren); he was probably mistaken since the former post belonged to the Chancellery whereas the latter was an appointment of the Secretariat. Since Cen was working in the Secretariat prior to this appointment, it is more logical to assume that he was transferred within the same department rather than to another branch of the government.

34. See QTS 2038/2 where Cen refers to himself as the "disgraced official."

35. QTS 2047/2.

36. Huan Tan (d. 56) opposed the Emperor Wu of Han's belief in prognostication and was demoted to magistrate of Liu'an. He died on the way.

37. Cen's poems give some indication of the approximate dates of these appointments. A composition addressed to Yan Wu (QTS 2085/5) when he was Metropolitan Prefect mentions that he himself was working in the Department of Personnel, of which the Bureau of Merit was a division. Since Yan held that office until the autumn of 763, Cen's tenure as Assistant Secretary of the Bureau of Merit can be placed to that year. By the following year he seemed to have received his promotion to Head of the Bureau of Forestry, for the preface to a composition by Yu Shao (QTW 428/5517) addressed Cen by that title and it is known from Yu's biography in JTS 188/3765 that he was away from Chang'an until 764.

38. This date is deduced from a poem sent to Vice-prefect Cheng (QTS 2031/1) where Cen notes that he received his appointment at the same time as Cheng's appointment to Shu; Cheng's appointment is dated from a reference by Dugu Ji (QTW 386/4977) to the eleventh month of 765.

39. QTS 2045/3 and 4.
40. QTS 2091/3.
41. QTS 2047/1.
42. See QTS 2028/2.
43. The title of this piece has also been given as "Zhao beike" (Summoning the northern visitor) and its authorship attributed to Dugu Ji (725-777).
44. Cen's last datable poem, a dirge to Pei Mian, is in QTS 2093/3. Du Fu's "Feast of Man" (QTS 2382/2) was inspired by finding a poem sent to him by Gao Shi shortly before the latter's death. (QTS 2218/2).
45. Wang Dang, Tang yulin (Forest of talk on the Tang) (Taipei: Shijie, 1962), 3/71.
46. See XTS 150/4810 and 142/4667.

Chapter Two
1. Du Que in his preface claims that he collected eight juan or fascicles of Cen Shen's works from the holdings of the poet's son, Cen Zuogong. By the Song, Du Que's original edition seemed to have been lost, for both the XTS 50/1603 and Zhao Gongwu (fl. 1144), in Junzhai Dushuzhi (SBCK ed.), 4/18, list Cen's works as contained in ten fascicles. Several printings of the poet's works were made during the Ming. In 1520 alone there was a total of three printings, two in Sichuan consisting of four and eight fascicles, respectively, and one in Jinan in seven fascicles. A copy of the

seven-fascicle edition belonging to Mr. Zhu of Xiaoshan was reprinted in the SBCK. The QTS edition of Cen's poetry was compiled from an unidentified eight-fascicle Ming edition. Numerically, the QTS contains eleven more poems than the SBCK edition; two of the poems (QTS 2106/6 and 2055/3), however, are given as one composition in the SBCK (2/29). The remaining ten pieces not found in the SBCK are QTS 2081/3, 2081/4, 2088/4, 2095/1, 2095/2, 2106/3, 2107/4, 2098/1, 2099/5, and 2100/1. Cen also left behind a negligible body of prose works: one fu and two epitaphs (QTW 358/4597). Another prose composition entitled "Summoning the Shu Visitor to Return" is attributed to both Cen and Dugu Ji.

    2. Shi poetry is usually divided into two broad categories: ancient-style (gutishi) verse dates from the 2nd century; it is a form with no fixed length or tone pattern and allows for rhyme change. Modern style (jintishi) consists of two major forms: (1) Regulated verse (lushi), developed in the Tang, is a poem of eight lines with a prescribed tonal pattern; it requires the use of a constant rhyme in the even-numbered lines as well as two pairs of antithetical couplets in the middle four lines. (2) The quatrain (jueju) is half the length of a regulated style poem and for the most part observes the same rules of tonal pattern and rhyme but not of antithesis. Some quatrains, however, do not subscribe to the rules of tonal pattern and are known as quatrains in the ancient mode (gufeng). In the Tang, characteristics of modern-style poetry were sometimes introduced into the gushi with the result that many gushi contain couplets or whole passages that conform to the lushi's tonal pattern and requirements for antithesis. All three forms are further divided into poems in the pentasyllabic and heptasyllabic lines (the gushi entertains lines of other lengths, but such poems are in the minority), with the caesura falling between the second and third syllables in pentasyllabic verse and between the fourth and fifth syllables in the heptasyllabic poem.

    Antithesis refers to the matching of either grammatical or semantic categories or both. Tonal pattern designates the fixed rules for tonal balance and contrast. These rules are the subject of a body-length study by Wang Li, Hanyu shilu xue (A study of Chinese prosody) (Shanghai: Jiaoyu chuban she, 1963).

    3. A celebrated example is the quatrain attributed to Jia Dao in QTS 6693/1.

4. The story of Fei Changfang is found in the Hou Hanshu (History of the later Han), 82/2743. For the allusion to Wang Qiao, see Hou Hanshu, 82/2712, see Xu Xiaomu ji (Collected works of Xu Xiaomu), (Changsha: Commercial Press, 1939), p. 5.

5. Lanka in line 1 refers to the Lankavatara Sutra, a discourse attributed to Sakyamuni, who was said to have delivered it on Mt. Lanka (modern Adam's Peak, Sri Lanka). Yingyang (line 2) is located near Yingling, Henan.

6. The Feng River runs into the Wei River near Chang'an.

7. Stone Gate (line 18) is a standard feature of the recluse's abode. For Zheng Yun, see Li Shan's note to Xie Huilian's "Autumn Thoughts" in WX 23/313; for Yan Guang, see Hou Hanshu, 83/2763.

8. Taibo is the name of several mountains; Cen is referring either to the Taiyi Peak, near Mei, Shaanxi, or the mountain in Xichuan, Henan, named after the former. Yangtao (line 10) is the Actinidia Chinensis.

9. For an example of a study of Tang poetic language based on modern linguistic approaches, see Kao Yu-kung and Mei Tsu-lin, "Syntax, Diction and Imagery in T'ang Poetry," Harvard Journal of Asiatic Studies 31 (1971): 49-136.

10. The lines read literally: rock spring dine fragrant stalk / Wine jar open new vat.

11. Li Jiayan, "Cen Shen xinian" (A chronological biography of Cen Shen), in Tangshi yenjiu lunwen ji (Hong Kong, 1970), p. 54, assigns the piece to 759-61 because the mountainous terrain suggests Guozhou to him.

12. See QTS 1267/4, 1276/5.

13. QTS 1624/3.

14. The anthology and nine others are published in one volume as Tangren xuan Tangshi (Tang selections of Tang poetry) (Beijing: Zhonghua, 1958).

15. There is a textual variant of four lines between the QTS (2030/3) and the Heyue yingling ji (p. 81) versions of the poem. Lines 9 and 10 of the text in the Tang anthology, translated here, are omitted in the QTS and replaced by four different lines. Qin Mountain is another name for Mt. Zhongnan, in the mountain range that spans southern Shaanxi and parts of Henan and Gansu; its highest peak is located south of Chang'an. The King of Qin (lines 8-9) may refer to the Shiji (Records of the historian), 81/1665, which tells of how he was outwitted by Lin Xiangru. When he insulted Lin's master, King Hui of Zhao, by demanding that he play the zither, Lin Xiangru avenged

his master by making the King of Qin beat the wine vat, a common practice in antiquity for accompanying a song. Zhang Zhongwei (line 15) went into reclusion with a Wei Jingqing and their abode was said to have been completely hidden behind artemisia plants. See Sanfu juelu zhu by Zhi Yu (Jin dynasty) (Yuhan shanfang edition).

16. Mt. Gou is located near Cen's home near Yanshi, Henan. The Green Creek mentioned here is not the same body of water as the one celebrated in Wang Wei's poem of that name, which is located in Shaanxi. Chao Fu and Xu You (line 9) were two recluses who were offered the throne by the legendary emperor Yao and turned it down.

17. Poems on history come under a variety of titles; the most common include "yonggu" (Song of Antiquity), "yongshi" (Song of History), "huaigu" (Cherishing Antiquity), "guyi" (Ancient Thoughts), as well as the names of historical personages and places. See Hans Frankel's study of this group of poems in The Flowering Plum and the Palace Lady (New Haven: Yale University Press, 1976), pp. 104-28.

18. See Shiji 58/883.

19. WX 16/211.

20. For the periodization of Tang poetry, see note 25, Chapter 5.

21. WX 45/635.

22. YFSJ, juan 28, vol. 7.

23. The Fu River is located west of Huaying, Shaanxi.

24. The origin of the association of the carp with letters is not clear; Wen Yiduo suggests that in ancient times, letters written on white silk were placed in wooden containers whose two halves were shaped like two flat carp fishes. See his Complete Works, 4:124.

25. WX 27/379.

26. A poem by Dugu Ji (QTS 2770/2), which accompanies this composition, addresses Cen as "Bureau Chief" (langzhong), which would place the composition of this poem at about 765. The stanzaic division in the translation of this and other poems marks the intervals dividing the changes of rhymes.

27. YFSJ, juan 34, vol. 7.

28. Jade Pass was located west of modern Dunhuang, Gansu, on the ancient route to the western region.

29. Weizhou refers to the area southwest of Longxi, Gansu. The Wei River flows from Niaoshu, Gansu, past Chang'an, and eventually joins the Yellow River. Qin and Yongzhou were ancient names for the Chang'an area.

30. Lucerne Beacon was one of five beacons beyond Jade Pass. Gourd River flows past the pass and was so named because the upper reaches of the river are narrow whereas the lower reaches broaden out.
31. See Jingjie xiansheng ji (Collected works of Mr. (Tao) Jingjie), with commentary by Tao Shu (Hong Kong: Taiping, 1964), 2/54.
32. Tangren xuan Tangshi, p. 81.
33. Fan Xi (Song dynasty), Duichuang yeyu (Nocturnal talks across the couch), 4/2b, in XLDSH, vol. 2.
34. Yuyin conghua (Collected comments of the fisherman-recluse) (Taipei: Shijie, 1961), vol. 2, 9/478.
35. For Iron Gate Pass, see the discussion of Poem 49, Chapter 4.
36. Jilian refers to the mountain range stretching westwards from Zhangyi, Gansu; it is also known as the Tianshan range. Yang Pass, southwest of Dunhuang, Gansu, was with Jade Pass, located on the main route connecting the Chinese empire and the western regions. Duling, located southwest of the western capital, was one of the twenty districts surrounding Chang'an which made up the Jingzhao or Capital Prefecture.

Chapter Three
1. See Morino Shigeo, "Ryō no bungaku no yūgisei" (Literary games of the Liang), Chūgoku chūsei bungaku kenkyū 6 (June 1967): 27-40.
2. The palace was completed by Gaozong in 634 on the eastern side of the imperial city. It stood in the foothills of the Longshou mountain; the elevation was deemed to have been beneficial to Gaozong's rheumatism. In the succeeding reigns it was also known as Penglai, Hanyuan, as well as Daming Palace. It was the principal palace of the Tang emperors.
3. See XTS 119/4298.
4. "Purple road" refers to the boulevards of the capital city. "Silver candle" is also a kenning for the moon. Jianzhang (line 4) refers to the palace located outside Chang'an, dating to 104 B.C., when it was built on the site of the old Boliang Tower. Phoenix Pond is another name for the Secretariat.
5. "Keeper of the cock" (line 1) refers to the guard charged with sounding the morning call from beyond Vermilion Bird Gate each day. "Immortal Palms" (line 5) belong to the statues of Taoist immortals, holding containers

for collecting the dew which was used for alchemical preparations. Imperial edicts (line 7) were issued on papers of black, red, blue, yellow, and white.

6. "Song of the Bright Spring" (line 8) is an allusion to Song Yu's "Responding to the King of Chu," where he claims that few can compose poems to match the ancient song "Bright Spring's White Snow." See WX 45/626.

7. See Mori Orai's notes in the Tangshi xuan pingshi (Selection of Tang poetry with critical commentary), comp. Li Panlong (1512-1570) (Hong Kong: Commercial Press, 1958), 4/414.

8. Siming shihua (Siming's comments on poetry), 3/12b, in XLDSH, vol. 4.

9. Tianzhitang shihua (Tianzhitang's comments on poetry), in Xuehai leibian, ed. Cao Qiuyue (Beijing: Wenyuan, 1964), 5/3056.

10. Chengzhai shihua (Chengzhai's comments on poetry), 3a, in XLDSH, vol. 1.

11. Shizhou shihua (Shizhou's comments on poetry), 1 (Yueyatang congshu ed.), p. 2731.

12. Shifajia shu (Discrimination of the masters on poetic rules), in Martin, p. 475.

13. Wang Li, Hanyu shilu xue, p. 52, claims that it was only in the Song and after that poems of accompaniment were required to observe the rhyme of the initial poem.

14. The tonal patterns of the Daming poems are given below. Where ao or tonal deviations occur, the orthodox tone is given in brackets, - represents the level tone; + designates the oblique tone; and R, the rhyme.

1. Jia Zhi

-(+)	+	-		-	+		+		-R
+(-)	-	-(+)		+	+		-		-R
+(-)	-	+		+	-		-		+
+	+	-		-	+		+		-R
+	+	-		-	+(-)		-(+)		-
-	-	-(+)		+	+		-		-R
+	+	-		-	+(-)		-(+)		+
-	-	+		+	+		-		-R

2. Wang Wei

+	+	-		-	+		+		-R
+(-)	-	-(+)		+	+		-		-R
+(-)	-	-(+)		+	-		-		+
+	+	-		-	+		+		-R
+	+	-		-	-		+		+

```
       -    -    +    +    +    -    -R
      -(+)  +    -         -(+)  +    +
      +(-)  -   -(+)  +    +     -    -R
```

3. Du Fu
```
       +    +   +(-)  -    -    +    +
      +(-)  -   -(+)  +    +    -    -R
       -    -    +    +    -    -    +
      -(+)  +    -    -    +    +    -R
      -(+)  +    -    -    -    +    +
       -    -   -(+)  +    +    -    -R
      +(-)  -    +    +    -    -    +
      -(+)  +    -    -   -(+)  +    -R
```

4. Cen Shen
```
       -    -    +    +    +    -    -R
      -(+)  +    -    -   -(+)  +    -R
      -(+)  +   +(-)  -    -    +    +
      +(-)  -   -(+)  +    +    -    -R
       -    -    +    +    -    -    +
       +    +    -    -    +    +    -R
       +    +   +(-)  -    -    +    +
       -    -    +    +    +    -    -R
```

15. Middle Chinese reconstructions are based on Hugh Stimson, T'ang Poetic Vocabulary (New Haven: Far Eastern Publications, 1976). These transcriptions are used only when the euphonic value of the word is under consideration. In other cases the standard pinyin romanizations appear.

16. Wang Li, Hanyu shilu xue, p. 101.

17. Xianyong shuoshi (Xianyong's talks on poetry), in QSH 991.

18. See note 9.

19. Shijing zonglun (General discourse in the area of poetry), 11b in XLDSH, vol. 5.

20. See Du Shaolong ji xiangzhu (The annotated poetry of Du Shaoling) (Beijing: Zhonghua, 1974), p. 92; Wang Li, Hanyu shilu xue, p. 168.

21. Shisou (The preserve of poetry) (Beijing: Zhonghua, 1958), 5/95.

22. For the custom of new jinshi holders signing their names at the stupa, see Li Zhao (fl. 806-820), Tang guoshi bu (Supplementary Tang history) (Shanghai: Guji, 1971), 1/29. Sun Zhu (1711-1778), in Tangshi sanbaishou jishi (Anthology of the 300 Tang poems with explanatory notes) (Taipei: Yiwen,

1977), 1/50, quotes a description of the temple by Wei Shu of the Tang in Liangjing xinji (New records of the two capitals).
23. Hung, Tu Fu, p. 72; Wen Yiduo, "Cen Jiazhou xinian kaozheng," p. 119, and Ruan Tingyu, in his chronology of Gao Shi in Gao Changshi shi jiaozhu (Annotated poetry of Gao Changshi) (Taipei: Zhonghua congshu bianshen weiyuan hui, 1965), p. 23, are in agreement about the dating of this suite to 752.
24. "Fragrant region" (line 1) translates the Buddhist term xiangjie, while "confused" is mian, and "aspect of differentiation," zhuxiang. In line 4, the stupa is referred to as the "power of the great" (dazhuang), the name of a hexagram from the Book of Changes which the "Appended Judgments" interpret in the following way: "In ancient times people dwelt in caves and lived in forests. The holy men of a later time made the change to buildings. At the top was a ridgepole and sloping down from it, there was a roof to keep off the wind and rain. They probably took this form from the hexagram, dazhuang." See R. Wilhelm, tr. The Book of Changes, rendered into English by Cary Baynes (New York: Bollingen Foundation, 1950), p. 199. "Windflapped" (pifu) in line 4 and "spirit invigorated" (shenwang) in line 8 appear in the Zhuangzi, chapters 3 and 14, respectively. See, Wang Xianqian, Zhuangzi jijie (The Zhuangzi with collected explanations) (Hong Kong: Zhonghua, 1960), pp. 19, 80. The Five Mounds (line 14) refer to the tombs of five Han emperors located outside Chang'an; Gaodi's at Changling, some thirty li north of the capital; Huidi's at Anling, approximately twenty li northeast; Jingdi's at Yangling, forty li east; Wudi's at Maoling, seventeen li northwest; and Zhaodi's at Pingling, located some twenty li northwest of the city. For Ruan Ji see Jinshu (History of the Jin), 49/1361. For Zhou Fang, see Hou Hanshu, 79/2559, and for Xie Lingyun, see Songshu (History of the Song), 53/1524-25.
25. "Teaching by symbols" (xiangjiao) in line 5 refers to Buddhism. The Jing waters (line 14) flow from two sources in Gansu into Shaanxi, joining the Wei River at Gaoling; they were said to have been as clear as the waters of the Wei were muddy. The yellow swan (line 21) is a mythical bird, the vehicle of immortal beings. For the Qin Mountain, see note 15, Chapter 2.
26. See Qianzhu Dushi (Qian's annotated Du Fu reader) (Beijing: Zhonghua, 1973), 1/18.
27. See WX 11/145.

28. For brief biographical entries of Chu Guangxi, see Ji Yougong (Song dynasty), Tangshi jishi (Record of events in Tang poetry) (Hong Kong: Zhonghua, 1972), 22/322, and TCZZ 1/18.

29. The Yichun Gardens (line 5) refer to the grounds of the imperial palace. Lake Kunming (line 6) was the artificial lake of great antiquity southwest of Chang'an which was filled up during the reign of Wenzong (827-840) and became arable land.

30. According to the standard Buddhist dictionaries, "palace of the gods" (line 2) translates the devapura or the six celestial worlds situated between earth and the Brahamalokas. "Sacred land" (line 5) is the abbreviation for chrxian shenzhou, an old kenning for the Chinese empire. "Within the pass" (line 16) refers to the land west of the Hangu Pass. "Good cause" (line 20) translates the Buddhist term shengyin while "way to awareness" translates juedao.

31. Xianyong shuoshi, p. 978.
32. Shifajia shu, p. 474.
33. QTS 1303/5.
34. See Frankel, The Flowering Plum and the Palace Lady, pp. 73-104.
35. The Shiji, 27/1289, refers to the mirages of the south while the jiaoren is mentioned in Ren Fang (Liang dynasty), Shuyi ji (Account of strange events), in Baizi chuan shu (Shanghai: Saoye shanfang, 1919), p. 43. The "Three Mountains" refer to three peaks south of Nanhai: Gan, Wushi, and Yuewang, as well as the mountains of Fairyland - Penglai, Yingzhou, and Fanghu.

36. For Weicheng or Wei Citadel, see note 25, Chapter 1. "Song of Wei Citadel" was the title of a popular parting song in Cen Shen's day. Ying (line 7) refers to the river which flows from Dengfeng, Henan, into the Sha River.

37. Baling was located beyond the Ba Gate or Blue Gate in the east side of Chang'an.
38. Kongqi shihua, 4a, in XLDSH, vol. 2.
39. Wang Changling's biographies are in JTS 190/5050, and XTS 203/5780.
40. QTS 1769/2.
41. The Huai (line 8) flows from Henan to Anhwei and Jiangsu. Spring Rich Islet (line 9) is on the Qiantang River. Xuzhou (line 12), one of the nine ancient geographical divisions, covers modern northwest Jiangxi, Shandong, and northeast Anhwei. Jingkou (line 17) refers to modern Zhenjiang, Jiangsu. "Sharing a coverlet" (line 16) is a

standard trope for intimate friendship.

42. The concluding sentiment echoes the last lines of "Watering My Horse at the Cavern by the Great Wall." See note 25, Chapter 2.

43. "Wuchang fish" (line 3) alludes to a folk song which circulated shortly after Sun Hao moved his capital from Jianye to Wuchang in 264 and which contained the couplet "I'd rather drink the waters of Jianye, / Then eat the fishes of Wuchang." For Baling, see note 37, and for Jilian, see note 36, Chapter 2. Shupu (line 10) was a game of military strategy played with dice; a description of this popular Tang game appears in Li Zhao's Tang guoshi bu, 3/61. Master Fei's appearance is a composite of many literary and historical descriptions of strong men; for example, see the description of Shun in Songshu, 27 (SBBY ed.), 2/13, of stalwart men in the Hou Hanshu, 24/853, and a description by Liang Jianwendi in Han Wei Liuchao baisanjia ji (Collected works of the authors of the Han, Wei and Six dynasties), comp. Zhang Pu (Taipei: Xinxing, n.d.), 10/2642.

44. The originality of Cen's farewell poetry is noted by Zhou Zuchuan in Sui Tang Wudai wenxue shi (Literary history of the Sui, Tang and Five dynasties) (Fuzhou: Fujian People's Publications, 1958), p. 38.

45. See Tangyin guiqian, 5/41.

46. For the Fire Mountains, see the discussion of Poem 51, Chapter 4. Chiting refers to the mountain located near Wuwei, Gansu and also a garrison near Hami. For Jade Pass, see note 28, Chapter 2. Jiaohe is the Chinese for the city of Yarkhoto in modern Xinjiang.

Chapter Four

1. The early Tang poet Shen Quanqi (d. 713) left a composition entitled "On Being Examined on 'Leaving the Frontier.'" See QTS 1034/5.

2. See Li Shutong, Tangshi kaobian (Critical examination of Tang history) (Taipei: Zhonghua, 1965), p. 57.

3. See Xinjiao zizhi tongjian zhu (Comprehensive mirror as an aid to government with revised annotations), comp. Sima Guang (1019-1086) (Taipei: Shijie, 1962), 215/6849.

4. QTS 2190/2.

5. See Denis Twitchett, ed., The Cambridge History of China (Cambridge, 1979), 3:367; Yang Shufan, Tangdai zhengzhishi (A history of Tang government regulations) (Taipei: Zhengzhong, 1967), p. 275.

6. See the works on the Tang material culture by Edward

Schafer, including The Golden Peaches of Samarkand (Berkeley: University of California Press, 1963).
7. QTS 2032/2.
8. QTS 2189/2.
9. QTS 2254 and 2292.
10. See Lu Kanru and Feng Yuanjun, Zhongguo shishi (A history of Chinese poetry) (Beijing: Zuojia, 1956), pp. 436-46; Liu Dajie, Zhongguo wenxue fadashi (A history of the development of Chinese literature) (Taipei: Zhonghua, 1966), pp. 417-26. For biographical notices of Cui Hao, see JTS 190/5049, XTS 203/5780, and TCZZ 1/17; for Wang Zhihuan, see Tangshi jishi, 26/394, and TCZZ 3/37; for Li Qi, see TCZZ 2/28.
11. The episode is found in Xue Yongruo, Jiyi ji (Record of strange events), in Lidai xiaoshi, comp. Li Shi (Shanghai: Hanfen lou photo, reprint of the Ming woodblock edition), 26/8b.
12. Tangren xuan Tangshi, p. 83.
13. See Tan Youxue, "Wang Changling xingnian kao" (A study of Wang Changling's chronology), in Wenxue yichan (Beijing: Zhonghua, 1963), pp. 174-92. See also note 39, Chapter 3.
14. See note 26, Chapter 1, and note 23, Chapter 3, for Gao Shi's biographies.
15. See Ueo Ryūsuke, "Shinshin no hensai shi" (Cen Shen's frontier poetry), in Mekada Makoto hakushi kanreki kinen Chūgokugaku ronshū (1964), p. 92.
16. See Tangyin guiqian, 10/79.
17. See Zhou Baoquan, ed., Sikong Tu shipin zhushi ji yiwen (Sikong Tu's classification of poetry with annotations and translation) (Hong Kong: Commercial Press, 1966), p. 40.
18. Canglang shihua (Canglang's comments on poetry), in Martin, p. 443.
19. See Tangyin guiqian, 10/78.
20. For the Long Mountain, see note 18, Chapter 1.
21. See YFSJ, juan 21, vol. 6.
22. See Wang Li, Hanyu shilu xue, p. 221.
23. See XTS 40/1046. For Iron Gate Pass (line 2), see the discussion of Poem 49, Chapter 4.
24. Mingshi (SBBY ed.) 329/12.
25. Aurel Stein, Serindia (Oxford: Clarendon Press, 1921), p. 1228.
26. Fuchang (line 2) is better known as Lake Lop Nor.
27. "Flowing sand" (line 7) is the name of several desert areas in the western region, including the great Takla Makan

Desert, south of Kucha.

28. Yin Mountain (line 1) spans Suiyuan, Chahar, and Jehol in the northeast and north-central frontiers of China. Annotators in general take "snowy lake" as referring to the snow covered region near the Pamirs rather than a real lake. XTS 436/7149, however, mentions a "Snow Lake" near Talas, some one hundred li from Lake Issyk-kul.

29. Yan Zhenqing's biographies are in JTS 128/3589 and XTS 153/4854.

30. For a description of this instrument, see the Wenxian tongkao (Comprehensive history of civilization), comp. Ma Duanlin (ca. 1250-1325) (Basic Sinological Series), 138/1224.

31. QTS 2217/3.

32. See Du Yu (735-812), Tongdian (Comprehensive institutes) (Basic Sinological Series), 193/1039.

33. See XTS 220/6186, and Kishibe Shigeo, Tangdai yinyweshi de yenjiu (A study of Tang music), tr. Liang Zaiping and Huang Zhiqiong (Taipei: Zhonghua, 1973), p. 538.

34. Arthur Waley, "A Chinese Poet in Central Asia," in The Secret History of the Mongols and Other Pieces (London, 1963), p. 40.

35. There was a Mt. Huamen (line 12) between Liangzhou and Zhangyi, Gansu.

36. The sense of langan (line 9) as railings of ice hanging from the cliffs is clear in poem 59. There are some textual variants on the measurement in the next line, among "hundred feet," "thousand feet," and "three hundred meters" (zhang); Stephen Owen in The Great Age of T'ang Poetry (New Haven, 1980), p. 377, argues that since all three refer to a negligible area, langan must describe depth rather than breadth. White grass (line 1) is a stock image of frontier poetry. For Luntai, see the discussion of Poems 53 and 54, Chapter 4, and for Tianshan, see the next poem.

37. Tianshan is the great mountain system of Central Asia, stretching from Russia into China. For Chiting (line 3) and Jiaohe (line 7), see note 46, Chapter 3. For Mt. Silver Desert (line 5), see the discussion of Poem 48, Chapter 4, and for Iron Gate Pass, note 23.

38. Cen observes in a note in the QTS edition that the carp (line 4) is the red carp. "Moon Cavern" (line 10) is a kenning for the western region.

39. See Lu Shiyong's comments in Shijing zonglun, 8b.

40. E. Eitel in Handbook of Chinese Buddhism (Amsterdam: Philo Press, 1970), 184b, glosses the Youbenlou as the Udumbara Tree of Buddhist writings, which is the

Ficus Glomerata. See G.A. Stuart, Chinese Materia Medica (Reprint ed. Taipei: Gudian, 1969), p. 175. For the Yang Pass (line 15), see note 36, Chapter 2.

41. The Pleiades (line 2) is the astronomical sign of the Tartar army; see Edward Schafer, Pacing the Void (Berkeley: University of California Press, 1977), p. 81. Quli (line 3) was a tribe based southeast of Luntai. A feather inserted on a military dispatch signified an emergency. The Altai, or Gold Mountain, is the northern branch of Tianshan and extends some one thousand miles from the Gobi to the western Siberian plains. For the "snow sea" and for Yin Mountain, see note 28. Sword River (line 13) refers to a river located east of Qingshan in modern Gansu. The exact location of Sand Mouth is unclear.

42. C.H. Wang, "Towards a Chinese Definition of Heroism," Journal of the American Oriental Society 95(1975):25-36.

43. Running Horse River is not readily identifiable; it may be the Kucha River mentioned in the Shuijing zhu (Classic of the rivers), chap. 2, as flowing east of Bugur. See Zhao Yiqing, ed., Shuijing zhushi (Annotated classic of the rivers) (photo, reprint of 1795 edition, Taipei: Huawen, 1970), 1/38. "Five petals" (line 13) is glossed in two possible ways: (1) a horse with spotted or mottled hide, hence dapple or piebald, (2) the contemporary custom of dressing the horse's mane into three or five sections to resemble flower petals. Jushi in the last line refers to the Karakhoja (Gaochang) tribe based near Turfan. In 638, it surrendered to the Chinese when its ruler, Qu Wentai, died of fright when he learned of the Chinese advance toward his land. Tang then annexed Karakhoja and renamed it Xizhou. See Twitchett, Cambridge History of China, p. 224.

44. See Shen Deqian, Tangshi biecai (Selections from Tang poetry) (Shanghai: Guji, 1979), 1/166; Wang Li, Hanyu shilu xue, p. 372.

45. Line 4 refers to the Han princess Wang Zhaojun, who was given in marriage to a Wusun chief and who is often depicted in paintings on horseback, holding a piba. For the location of Jade Pass, see note 28, Chapter 2, and for Jiaohe, note 46, Chapter 3.

46. Xiao Pass (line 2) was located at Guyuan, Gansu. You (line 5) refers to modern Hebei, and Bin, to modern Shanxi; these northern regions are associated with knights-errant.

47. Weiyang, dating to the Han dynasty, was a palace in

northwest Chang'an. Unicorn Chamber, also dating to the Han, contained portraits of distinguished officials and was used to honor meritorious public servants. Ershi (line 4) is the title of the Han general Li Guangli (d. 90 B.C.), bestowed upon him in 104 B.C. by the Emperor Wu.

48. Loulan is the Chinese name for Kroraina, a Central Asian state of Han times, while Rush Lake (line 3) is Lop-nor, and Scallion Mountain (line 4), the Pamirs. For "Moon Cavern," see note 38.

49. Legend claims that when Zhang Hao was serving as premier of Liang, he saw a magpie metamorphosed into a stone which, when broken, yielded a seal engraved with the words "seal of loyalty and filial piety."

50. Fish Lake (line 3) is the Chinese name for Lake Alakul, while Dragon Dunes (line 4) is Kumtagh.

51. For Tianshan, see note 37.

52. Beiting is the Chinese name for Besbaliq. West Lake (line 5) is better known as Qinghai or Lake Kokonor. The "two courts" (line 5) refer to the schism of the Xiongnu tribe during the Han into two divisions under separate leaders. A similar schism took place among the western Turks during the Tang. For Yin Mountain, see note 28, and for Dragon Dunes (line 10), see note 50.

53. Gai Tinglun's career at Hexi is mentioned in the Zizhi tongjian, 219/7015. The SBCK edition of Cen's poetry identifies General Gai as Gai Jiayun; Wen Yiduo has shown that Jiayun was not employed by 756. See Wen Yiduo, "Cen Jiazhou," p. 139. "Bearer of the Golden Apotropaion" (line 3) is the title of the Chief of Police of Metropolitan Chang'an during the Han; the bird was carried on a staff held before the emperor when he was traveling to ward off evil. In line 4, the Chinese foot (chi), measuring approximately one-third of a meter, is a little shorter than the English foot. General Gai was, therefore, well over six feet. The dictionaries gloss Rong (line 7) as the western tribes, while Hu were the northern barbarians. "Phoenix Fledgling" (line 20) is the title of the ancient song that, according to the YFSJ, juan 44, vol. 9, was lost after the Liang dynasty. For Qin Lofu, see note 22, Chapter 2. Casting complete black at shupu (line 25) meant a win (see note 43, Chapter 3). Xianyang (see note 25, Chapter 1) refers to the capital and the last statement expresses longing for home.

54. Regional Commander Wei was Wei Boyu, whose biography is in JTS 115/3378 and who was stationed in Anxi before serving in Shaanzhou from 758-61. "Phoenix city" (line 9) is a poetic epithet for the capital city. The "triple mane" (line 14) describes the contemporary equine fashion, whereby the horse's mane was dressed in the "three petals" or the "five petals" style. See note 43, and Bo Juyi's description in QTS 5064/2. For Weiyang (line 21), see note 47.

55. For "flowing sand" (line 6), see note 27, and for Jiaohe, note 46, Chapter 3. "Blood sweating breed" (line 12) refers to the famous steeds first introduced to China from Ferghana. Horizontal Gate (line 16) was the extreme western gate of Chang'an.

56. Xianyong shuoshi, p. 984.

Chapter Five
1. QTS 2059/3.
2. QTS 2259/1.
3. QTS 2261/2.
4. QTS 2427/2.
5. Jian'an (196-220) is the reign title of the Emperor Xian of Han. In poetry it refers to a group of poets who clustered around the court of Cao Cao in the state of Wei around 208. The most distinquished of the group were members of the Cao family: Cao Cao himself (155-220), his sons, Cao Pei (187-226) and Cao Zhi (192-232), perhaps the greatest of the Jian'an poets. Seven other literati of Cao's court became known in literary history as the Jian'an Pleiad: they are Kong Yong, Chen Lin, Wang Can, Xu Gan, Ruan Yu, Ying Chang, and Liu Zhen. Living in an age of chaos following the dissolution of the Han dynasty, the Jian'an poets evoked the suffering they saw around them with realism and with what is traditionally described as a sense of noble fortitude.

6. See note 14, Chapter 2.

7. See the studies of this collection by Nakazawa Mareo, "Kagaku eireishū kō" (A study of the Heyue yingling ji), in Gumma Daigaku kiyō 1 (1951), and Wang Yunxi, "Shi Heyue yingling ji xu lun Sheng Tang shige" (Notes on the preface of the Heyue yingling ji as a means of studying High Tang poetic structure, in Tangshi yenjiu lunwen ji (Beijing: Renmin wenxue, 1959), pp. 26-37.

8. Tangyin guiqian, 10/78.

9. Tangshi pinhui (Collected classification of Tang poetry)

(Taipei: Commercial Press, 1976).
10. Canglang shihua, p. 452.
11. Wenxin diaolong (The carved dragon in the heart of literature), annotated by Fan Wenlan (Beijing: Renmin, 1978), 6/66.
12. Tangyin guiqian, 5/41; TCZZ 3/37.
13. Tangyin guiqian, 9/71.
14. The shihua record such extreme instances of the appreciation of isolated couplets, apart from the merits of the whole poem, as men who were remembered by a single couplet or who were given agnomens after a particularly felicitous phrase. See Yuan Mei (1716-1798), Jianzhu Suiyuan shihua (Annotated Suiyuan's comments on poetry), annotated by Lei Jin (Taipei: Dingwen, 1974), 1/4 and 3/7. See also W.L. Wong, "Selection of Lines in Chinese Poetry Talk Criticism," New Asia Academic Bulletin 1(1978): 33-44.
15. Xu Ju, Shiwu yuanshi (On the origin of things); quoted in Shi Maoqing, Cen Shen yenjiu (A study of Cen Shen) (Taipei: Commercial Press, 1971), p. 91. The lines are from QTS 2105/1 and 2059/1.
16. Beijiang shihua (Beijiang's comments on poetry) (CSJC ed.) 5/57.
17. Shuoshi zuiyu (Annual remarks on poetry), 1, in QSH 538. The lines are in QTS 2078/2.
18. Xianyong shuoshi, p. 999. The couplet is in QTS 2100/4.
19. Ibid, p. 984.
20. Yuyin conghua, vol. 2, 9/478. The couplet by Meng Haoran is in QTS 1630/4.
21. Yanzhou shihua (Yanzhou's comments on poetry), in Martin, p. 230.
22. Xianyong shuoshi, 984.
23. Bao Zhao is generally acknowledged as an early master of the heptasyllabic ancient style poem. In contrast to the formal and elegant compositions of his contemporaries, Bao's works are described by Du Fu (see QTS 2395/3) as strong and untrammeled and as anticipating the genius of Li Bo.
24. QTS 1670/1.
25. Scholars since the Song have divided Tang poetry into three or four periods. Ouyang Xiu and Song Ji in XTS 201/5727 and Yao Xuan (968-1020) in Tangwen Cui (Collection of Tang literature) (SBCK edition), p. 3, propose a division into Early Tang (618-713), High Tang (713-806), and Late Tang (806-910). During the Yuan and Ming

dynasties some scholars argued that there were sufficient changes within the middle period to warrant a further division; Gao Bing in the preface to Tangshi pinhui, p. 1; Xu Shizeng (fl. 1554) in Wenti mingbian (Discrimination of literary forms) (Hong Kong: Taiping, 1965), p. 106; and others advocate dividing Tang poetry into four periods: (1) Early (618-713); (2) High (713-766); (3) Middle (766-826); (4) Late (826-910). Proponents of the four periods are not in complete agreement about the exact date marking the shift from Middle to Late Tang and place it anywhere between 821 and 846.

26. Wenxin diaolong zhu, 29/518.

27. As the poems of the Shijing are anonymous, Qu Yuan (343?-278), the author of the "Lisao," is considered the earliest known poet. Song Yu was his disciple and successor in the sao mode. Qi and Liang were two of the Six Dynasties.

28. See the SBCK edition of Cen's works, p. 56.

29. Shijing zonglun, 8b.

30. Tangyin guiqian, 10/79.

31. Ibid, 3/20.

32. Yuanshi: waipan (On the origin of poetry: additional chapter), in QSH 604.

33. Yiyuan zhiyan (Comprehensive remarks on the garden of letters), 4/3b, in XLDSH, vol. 4.

34. Yuanshi: waipian, p. 604. The lines are in QTS 2096/3.

35. Yifu xieyu lunshi (Additional discourse on poetry from the garden of letters), in Martin, p. 498.

36. Wenxin diaolong zhu, 29/519.

37. Ibid, 28/514.

38. See Hu Zhenheng's remarks in Tangyin guiqian, 28/240.

39. Beside the excursion to the Temple of Compassionate Mercy, there seems to have been at least one other occasion when Gao Shi and Cen Shen were at the same party; there are farewell poems by both men to a certain Li Zhu on the occasion of his departure for the south. See QTS 2034/3 and 2239/1.

40. See Yiyuan zhiyan, 4/4b; Tangshi pinhui, p. 23; Tangshi biecai, 1/166.

41. Yiyuan zhiyan, 4/3b.

42. Tangyin guiqian, 9/72.

43. Ibid, 5/41.

44. Shizhou shihua, 1/7.

45. Tangyin guiqian, 10/79

46. Yuanshi: waipian, p. 604

47. See the comments in Tangshi xuan pingshi, 4/414.
48. See Sanguo zhi (Annals of the three kingdoms), 1/32.
49. This episode is recorded in the Sanguo zhi, 54/1262.
50. See Li Shangyin's poem "Without Title" in QTS 6168/6.
51. In Song Yu's "Gaotang fu" (WX 19/249), which describes the union of the spirit of Mt. Wu and the King of Chu, the spirit had described herself in a celebrated line as "a morning cloud at dawn, the rushing rain at dusk."
52. See Zhongguo shishi, 436; Zhongguo wenxue fadashi, p. 400.
53. See my Kao Shih (Boston, 1979).
54. See Owen, The Great Age of T'ang Poetry, p. 106.

Selected Bibliography

Primary Sources
(Editions of Cen Shen's works are only those generally available in recent reprintings.)
Quan Tangshi, juan 198-201. Compiled in 1705-6.
Cen Jiazhou ji. SBCK edition. Copy of the Ming woodblock edition of 1520 in seven fascicles or juan.
Cen Jiazhou shiji. Basic Sinological Series in seven fascicles.

Secondary Sources

In Chinese
Cao Jiping. "Cen Shen shengniande tuice" (Deducing the date of Cen Shen's birth). Tangshi yenjiu lunwen ji. Beijing: Zhonghua, 1959. pp. 70-73. Presents textual evidence that Cen Shen was born in 714.
Dong Shou. "Cen Jiazhou songren zhuodi shi chongfu" (Repetition in Cen Shen's poems presented to successful examination candidates). Dalu zazhi 2, No. 1 (1951):33.
He Changqun. "Lun Tangdaide biansai shi" (On the frontier poetry of the Tang). In: Tangshi yenjiu lunwen ji. Edited by Zhou Kangxie. Hong Kong: Zhongwen shudian, 1971, pp. 200-208. A short but useful essay on this important body of Tang poetry.
Huang Lanbo. "Du Cen Shen 'Baixue ge song Wu panguan" (A reading of Cen Shen's "Song of the White Snow: Upon Escorting Administrative Officer Wu"). Yuwen xuexi 24-26 (1955):24-26. A brief but perceptive analysis of one of Cen Shen's most celebrated poems.
Lai Hanchui and Lin Nan. "Cen Shen shi shi gesong wugongde ma?" (Is Cen Shen's poetry a celebration of martial exploits?). In: Tangshi yenjiu lunwen ji. (Beijing, Renmin, 1959). pp. 64-69.
Lai Yihui. "Cen Shen nianpu" (A chronological biography of Cen Shen). Lingnan xuebao 1, No. 2 (1940). Argues for placing the poet's birth at 718.

Li Jiayan. "Cen Shen xinian" (A chronological biography of Cen Shen), In: Tangshi yenjiu lunwen ji Hong Kong: Zhongguo yuwen xueshe, 1970, pp. 43-47. A supplement to Wen Yiduo's chronology of the poet's works.

Lin Maoxiong. "Cen Jiazhou shi jiaozhu" (The poetry of Cen Jiazhou with annotations). M.A. thesis, Institute of Chinese Studies, National Normal University, Taipei, 1971.

Liu Kaiyang. "Luetan Cen Shen he tade shi" (A brief discussion of Cen Shen and his poetry). In: Wenxue yichan xuanji. 2d edition. Beijing: Zuojia, 1957, pp. 42-57. An intelligent essay on Cen's works with the emphasis upon his frontier poetry.

Ruan Tingyu. "Cen Jiazhou jizhuanben xulu" (A list of editions of Cen Shen's works). Shumu jikan 10, No. 3 (1976): 63-78.

———. "Gao Changshi Cen Jiazhou qi ren yu shi zhi pingyu" (Critical remarks on Gao Changshi and Cen Jiazhou, the men and the poetry). Dalu zazhi 37, No. 10 (1978): 323-334. A compilation of critical remarks on Gao Shi and Cen Shen from the traditional treatises on poetry.

Shen Yucheng et al. "Lun Sheng Tangde biansai shi" (On the frontier poetry of the High Tang). In: Wenxue yichan 3 (1957): 59-78. An informative article, although the critical insights are somewhat distorted by the Marxist emphasis.

Shi Moqing. Cen Shen yenjiu (A study of Cen Shen). Taipei: Commercial Press, 1971. A study of the poet's life, poetry, and the traditional critical responses to his works.

Su Yinghui. "Bu Tangshu Cen Shen zhuan" (A biography of Cen Shen, supplementing the Tang histories). In: Dalu zazhi 17, No. 1 (1958): 7-10.

Sun Shushan. "Sheng Tang biansai shiren Cen Shen zhi yenjiu" (A study of the High Tang frontier poet, Cen Shen). M.A. thesis, Institute of Chinese Literature, National Fujen University, Taipei, 1971. Presents a new piece of evidence which may put Cen's death to 777.

Wen Yiduo. "Cen Jiazhou xinian kaozheng" (Textual evidence for Cen Jiazhou's chronological biography). In: Complete Works. Shanghai:

Kaiming shuju, 1948, 3:102-42. The seminal
chronology of Cen Shen's life and works.
Yang Yingshen. Gao Shi yu Cen Shen (Gao Shi and
Cen Shen). Shanghai: Commercial Press, 1935.
A comparative study of the two poets; follows
received opinion and offers little new critical
insights.

In Japanese
Matsueda Shigeo. "Futatabi Shinshin no 'Koka no uta'
ni tsuite - 'Kimi mizu,' 'Kimi kikazu,' kō"
(On Cen Shen's "Song of the Tartar Pipe" -
another study of the phrases "Don't you see?"
and "Don't you hear?"). Jimmongaku hō 36
(1973): 5-9.
Nakano Miyoko. "Shinshin no saigai shi" (Cen Shen's
poetry of the frontier). Nihon Chūgokugakkai hō
12 (1960):38-55. A discussion of four recurrent
images in Cen's frontier poetry.
Sugaya Shōgo. "Shinshin no koshi ni tsiute" (On
Cen Shen's ancient style poetry). Shinagaku
kenkyū 24 (1960):152-62. A study of the
prosody of Cen's ancient style poetry.
Suzuki Shūji. "Shinshin no shōgai to Toho -
Tōshijin no denki to sakuhin" (Cen Shen's life
and Du Fu - the Tang poet's biography and work)
Kambun Kyōshitsu 88 (1968): 7-15.
Suzuki Torao. "Shinkashū no shi" (The poetry of
Cen Jiazhou). Shinagaku 8, No. 1 (1935):1-13.
Ueo Ryūsuke. "Shinshin no hensai shi" (Cen Shen's
frontier poetry). Mekada Makoto Hakushi
kanreki kinen Chūgokugaku ronshū (1964):
91-114. A study of the geography of Cen's
frontier poetry.
____. "Shinshin no shi to seiiki" (Cen Shen's
poetry and the western regions). Kambun
Kyōshitsu 71 (1965):16-23.

In English
Chan, Marie. Kao Shih. Boston: Twayne
Publishers, 1978.
Hung, William. Tu Fu: China's Greatest Poet.
Cambridge, Mass: Harvard University Press,
1952. Still the most comprehensive biography
of Du Fu in English.

Selected Bibliography

Miao, Ronald C. "T'ang Frontier Poetry: An Exercise in Archetypal Criticism." Tsing hua Journal of Chinese Studies 10, No. 2 (1974):114-40.
Owen, Stephen. The Great Age of T'ang Poetry. New Haven: Yale University Press, 1980. Contains a stimulating chapter on Cen Shen.
Twitchett, Denis, ed. The Cambridge History of China, volume 3: Sui and T'ang China. Cambridge: Cambridge University Press, 1980. Chapter 4 on foreign relations in the reign of Taizong by Howard J. Wechsler, and Chapter 7 on Xuanzong by Denis Twitchett, offer the best background in English to Cen Shen's age.
Waley, Arthur. "A Chinese Poet in Central Asia." In The Secret History of the Mongols and Other Pieces. London: George Allen and Unwin, 1963. First published in 1951, this is the earliest essay on Cen Shen in English. Waley discusses Cen's frontier life and works; his opinions are sometimes biased and oftentimes in error, but the essay is still eminently readable.

Index

A Jiao, 31
Altai Mountain, 95, 97
An Lushan, 8, 30, 38, 44, 47, 73, 107, 109
An Sishun, 6
Ancient style poetry (gutishi), 18, 23
Antithesis, 23, 50, 80, 87, 96, 98, 102
Anxi, 6, 7, 8, 70, 77, 78, 82, 101

Baling, 65, 67, 70
"Ballad of the Army carts" (Bingju xing), 74
Bao Zhao, 111, 116
Beiting (Bashbeliq), 7, 9, 102, 109
Bian Gong, 118
Blue Gate, 69, 70
Bo Juyi, 43
"Boliang Terrace," 98
Book of Changes, 54
Boudoir lament (gui yuan), 20, 75

Cao Cao, 127-29
Caidiao ji, 112
Cen Changqian, 1
Cen Kuang, 2
Cen Wenben, 1
Cen Xi, 1, 3
Cen Zhi, 1, 2
Chang Jian, 113
Chang Kun, 17, 18
Chang'an, 4, 6, 7, 10, 11, 14, 16, 17, 37, 38, 53, 64, 72, 78, 86, 87, 88, 121
Changmen Palace, 31
"Chant of Longtou" (Longtou yin), 79
Chu Guangxi, 7, 44, 53, 58-59
Charchans, 95, 100
Chen Zi'ang, 114, 116
Chengdu, 16, 17
Chiting, 70
Chou Zhao'ao, 52
Chronicle annal (nianpu), 20
Cloud End Monastery, 5, 29
Complete Tang Poetry (Quan Tangshi) 19, 35, 72, 75, 79
Coleridge, Samuel Taylor, 37
Couplet (poetic), 50, 52, 97, 98, 114, 124, 125, 126; see also antithesis
Cui Hao, 75, 112
Cui Ning, 17
Cui Youfu, 17, 18

Daliang, 3
Daming Palace, 11, 44, 45, 58, 71, 102
Dark Horse Citadel, 86, 87
Dezong, 16
Dongting, Lake, 41
Dou Jian, 33
Double Ninth Festival, 11, 38
Dragon Dunes (Kumtagh), 101, 102, 103
Du Fu, 2, 3, 4, 6, 7, 9,

11-12, 13, 17, 44, 46, 47, 48, 49, 51-52, 53, 55-58, 59, 61, 71, 74, 105, 107, 108, 111, 112, 113, 117-18, 121
Du Hongjian, 16
Duling, 41
Du Que, 2, 14, 17, 30, 111, 112, 113, 116, 118

"Entering the Frontier" (Ru sai), 72, 78
Empress Wu (Wu Zhao), 1
"Eye" of the poetic line, 40, 114

Fang Guan, 12
Fei Changfang, 21, 109
Fen River, 32
Feng River, 23
Feng Changqing, 7, 8, 16 73, 82, 95, 97, 99, 100, 101, 102, 115
Fenggu, 114, 116, 120
Fengxiang, 9
Fengyi, 5
Feng Yuanjun, 130
Ferghana, 104
"Fighting South of the Citadel" (Zhan chengnan), 72
Fire Mountains, 8, 70, 71, 81, 82
Fish Lake (Lake Alakul) 101, 102
Five Mounds, 54, 55, 59, 60
Folk Songs, 36, 66; See also yuefu
Frankel, Hans, 62, 64
Frontier poetry, 20, 27, 72-108, 115

Fu (prose-poem), 3, 31, 57, 65
Fu River, 32, 33, 34
Fuchang (Lake Lopnor), 81
Fufeng, 123

Gai Tinglun, 8, 104, 110
Gao Bing, 113, 121
Gaoguan, 4
Gao Shi, 6, 7, 11, 44, 45, 53, 54-55, 61, 73, 74, 75, 87, 111, 112, 113, 118, 120-22, 123-27, 129, 130
Gao Xianzhi, 6, 7, 8, 73, 77, 107
Gaozong (Li Zhi), 53
Gaozu (Li Yuan), 72
Geshu Han, 73, 75
Gou Mountain, 30
Guozhou, 12, 14, 32, 123, 126

Handan, 3
Hangu Pass, 123, 124
Hanshi waizhuan, 57
Hanyang, 67, 68
Han Yu, 121
Han Zun, 22
Helong, 84
Heptasyllabic verse, 19, 97, 113, 114, 119, 137n2
He Sun, 111, 116
Hexi, 6, 75, 104
Heyue yingling ji, 29, 39, 112, 113, 116, see also Yin Fan
High Tang Poetry, 27, 32, 113, 116, 121, 151n25

Hong Liangji, 114
Hot Lake, 92, 93
Hot Springs, 56
Hu Prefecture, 4
Hu Yinglin, 52, 122
Hu Zhenheng, 113, 114, 118, 121, 122
Hu Zi, 40, 115, 120
Huamen Mountain, 88
Huai River, 66
Huazhou, 12
Huan Tan, 14
Huang Zhe, 65

Iron Gate Pass, 40, 41, 71, 79, 80, 91
Issyk-kul Lake, 92; see also Hot Lake

Jade Pass, 37, 99, 104
Jasper Pond, 56
Ji River, 65
Jia Ceng, 44
Jia Zhi, 11, 44, 45, 48, 49, 51
Jian'an (reign era), 112, 113, 114, 116
Jiang Hou, 23
Jiangning, 65, 66
Jianwen, Emperor or Liang (Xiao Gang), 117
Jianzhang Palace, 45
Jiaohe (Yarkhoto), 71, 99, 107
Jiaoren, 63
Jiazhou, 16, 17
Jilian, 41, 67
Jing (external scene), 62, 122
Jinshi (presented scholar), 1, 3, 4, 53, 72
Jinye Quarters, 53
Jiuquan, 41
Jixi, 82
Jushi, 98, 99

Kaiyuan (reign era), 3, 47, 110, 111, 117, 129, 130
Kangkai, 113
Karashahr, 79, 80
Kess (tribe), 87
Khitans, 72
Knight-errant (yuxia), 55, 68
Koreans, 72
Kucha, 6, 78
Kumeah, 87
Kunlun Mountain, 56, 84, 85

Lady Yang (Yang Guifei), 56
Lantian, 5
"Leaving the Frontier" (chu sai), 74, 88
Li Bo, 2, 3, 9, 39, 47, 65, 112, 113, 116, 118, 121
Li He, 114
Li Ling, 121
Li Mountain, 56
Li Qi, 75, 99, 100, 112, 113
Li Rihua, 47, 50
"Lisao," 9, 39; see also Qu Yuan

Index

Li Yi, 119
Liang dynasty, 117, 118
Liangzhou, 16
Liaodong, 85, 87
Linked pearl line, 23
Liu Changqing, 2, 3
Liu Xie, 109, 113, 116, 120; see also Wenxin diaolong
Liu Wu, 31
Longbiao, 65
Long, Mt., 7, 77, 84, 85
Long Waters, 77
Lopnor Lake, 81
Loulan (Kroraina), 84, 85, 100
Lucerne Beacon, 38
Luguang Lodge, 80
Lu Kanru, 130
Lu Shang (Taigong wang), 125, 126
Lu Shiyong, 51, 118
Luzhou, 17, 109
Luntai (Bugur), 7, 82, 83, 89, 91, 95, 96, 97, 102

Maimargh (tribe), 87
Mei Sheng, 31
Meipi Lake, 4
Meng Haoran, 2, 29, 40, 110, 111, 112, 115, 121, 129
Meng Jiao, 121
Meng Ruqing, 65
Mt. Silver Desert (Kumush), 79, 80, 91
"Mt. Yi Inscription," 98
Mu, King of Zhou, 56

"Mulberry by the Path" (Moshan can), 33
Nanhai, 62
New Criticism, 114

Opening Line (in poetry), 32, 51, 52, 60, 115
Owen, Stephen, 130

Palace style poetry (gongti shi), 20, 32, 111, 116, 117, 124
Pan Creek, 123, 125
Parrot Island, 68
Parting, 32, 43, 61-67, 124, 125
Pei Mian, 17
Pentasyllabic line, 19, 40, 113, 137n2
Phoenix Mountain, 68
"Phoenix Fledgling," 104
Piba, 89, 99
"Plucking the Lotus," 8, 88
"Plum Blossom Falling," 8, 86, 88
Poetic syntax, 26, 125

Qi dynasty, 117, 118
Qian Qianyi, 56
Qin Lofu, 33, 34, 104
Qin Mountain, 29, 84, 85
Qin Shihuangdi, 98
Qing (emotion), 62
Quli, 95
Qurug Tag Mountain, 81
Quatrain (jueju), 19, 101, 102

Qu Yuan, 9, 117; see
 also Lisao

Reclusion, 2, 20-30,
 91
Reed pipe, 85
Regulated poetry
 (lushi), 19, 83,
 137n2
Rhyme, 35, 43, 48, 80
Rongzhou, 17, 109
Ruan Ji, 55
Running Horse River,
 97
Rush Lake, 100; see
 also Lopnor Lake
Russet Slope, 91

Sand Mouth, 95, 96
Sanyun xiaolu, 80
Scallion Mountain
 (Pamir range), 101
Shao Hao, 56
Shaoshi, 2, 21
Shen Deqian, 98, 115,
 120, 121
Shen Yue, 111, 116,
 117
Shi Buhua, 50, 60,
 108, 115, 120
Shi Chaoyi, 16
Shi poetry, 76, 96
Shihua (Talks on
 poetry), 122, 123
Shiji, 63
Shijing, 36, 57,
 72, 117, 124
Shipin, 112; see
 also Zhong Hong
Shun, 56
Shupu, 8, 67, 105
Sikong Tu, 76
Sima Chengzhen, 2

Sima Xiangru, 31
Six dynasties poetry,
 112, 115, 116, 117,
 118
Song Mountain, 2
Song Yu, 117
Stein, Aurel, 80
Su Wu, 121
Sun Quan, 128
Suzong (Li Yu), 9,
 11, 44, 51, 108
Sword River, 95, 96

Taibo Mountain, 26,
 82
Taiping Princess, 1
Taizong (Li Shimin),
 53, 56
Talas, 7
Tao Qian, 4, 23, 38
Tarim River, 81
Temple of Compas-
 sionate Mercy, 7,
 53
Tendril Slope, 21,
 22
Tianbao (reign era),
 3, 72, 74, 129, 130
Tianshan Mountain, 9,
 84, 89, 91, 92, 102,
 103
Tibetans, 72, 74
Tonal compensation
 (jiu), 48-50
Tonal deviation
 (ao), 48-50
Turfen, 81
Turfen Depression, 8,
 81, 82
Turks, 72
Tuyouhun (tribe), 72
Twirl dance (huxuan),
 8, 86

Index

Unicorn Chamber, 100
Vermilion Bird Gate, 53
Waley, Arthur, 87
Wang Can, 57
Wang Changling, 2, 3, 65, 66-67, 68, 75, 99, 100, 112, 113
Wang, C.H., 96
Wang Dang, 17
Wang Li, 49, 52, 98
Wang Qiao, 21
Wang Shimao, 119
Wang Shizhen, 119, 122
Wang Wei, 3, 11, 23, 28-29, 44, 45, 47, 48, 49, 50, 61, 93, 110, 112, 113, 119, 121, 129
Wang Zhihuan, 75
War, 27, 72-73, 96, 98, 107, 108, 109, 115
"Waters of Longtou," 79
"Watering my horse at the cavern by the Great Wall," 34
Wei Citadel, 64
Wei Hu, 112
Wei River, 26, 37
Wei Zhuang, 112
Weiyang Palace, 100
Wen, King of Zhou, 125
Wenxin diaolong, 113; see also Liu Xie
Wenyang, 65

Weng Fanggang, 47, 122
West Lake (Kokonor), 102
White Wolf River, 86, 87
Wild goose, 40, 62, 123, 124
Willow, 62, 91
"Willow Branch," 72, 86
Wu, Emperor of Han, 25, 31, 32, 98
Wu Yun, 111, 116
Wuchang, 67, 68
Wuwei, 6, 82

Xi He, 56
Xiang, Ladies of the, 5
Xiang River, 41
Xianyang, 10, 77, 78, 105
Xiao Pass, 84, 85, 100
Xiao Zhi, 91
Xie Lingyun, 55
Xie Tiao, 111
Xie Zhen, 47
Xin Wenfang, 114, 121, 129
Xiongnu, 72
Xizhou (Qoco), 78
Xu Ju, 114
Xu Yi, 115
Xuanzong (Li Longji), 1, 43, 56, 72, 74, 107
Xuzhou, 66, 78
Xue Ju, 7, 44, 53

Yan Guang, 25
Yan Yu, 76, 113, 121

Yan Zhenqing, 84
Yanshi, 21, 22, 30
Yang Pass, 41, 74
Yang Wanli, 47
Yang Yuan, 62
Yang Zai, 47, 61, 62, 69
Ye (city), 127
Ye Xie, 119, 122
Yixi (Hami), 7, 9
Yin Fan, 39, 65, 75, 112, 114, 116, 117, 129; see also Heyue yinglingji
Yin Mountain, 83, 92, 95, 102
Ying River, 64
Yingyang, 20, 22, 23
You, 100
Youbenluo flower, 94
Youxuan ji, 112
Yu Xin, 117
Yuan Zhen, 43
Yuefu, 10, 113; see also folk songs

Zhang Zhongwei, 30
Zheng Yun, 25
Zhong Hong, 112; see also Shipin
Zhongnan Mountain, 4, 5, 24, 25, 29
Zhou Fang, 54
Zhou Yu, 128
Zhuangzi, 54
Zhuge Liang, 2
Zushen, 61
Zu Yong, 112

THE LIBRARY
ST. MARY'S COLLEGE OF MARYLAND
ST. MARY'S CITY, MARYLAND 20686